Godly Whispers

A 90-Day Devotional To Help You
Recover From Your Spouse's Affair

By:

Marsha Rozalski

D1473718

The Fine Print

Godly Whispers – A 90-day devotional to help you recover from your spouse's affair

For information about Marsha Rozalski:

marsharozalski@godlywhispers.com
www.godlywhispers.com

First Edition Written by Marsha Rozalski
Cover Design by Greg Raymond
Edited by Elizabeth Kennedy
Author Photo by Sue Culver

ISBN: 978-0-615-30649-0

Dedication

This book is dedicated to all those who have ever been devastated by the effects of infidelity. May you find comfort and healing within the pages of this book.

And to Elizabeth, for without her support, love, understanding and undying friendship I probably would have never written this book.

And to my husband, who has repeatedly shown me how much he loves and cherishes me. Thank you for all your love and support in helping make all my dreams come true. I truly love and adore you!

Table of Contents

1. When Life as You've Known It Has Ended 16
2. Shock 18
3. Why Lord? 20
4. The Level of Pain 22
5. Call upon a Friend 24
6. Let the Church Help You 26
7. You Need Friends 28
8. Where is God? 30
9. Overwhelmed? 32
10. Is This Really Happening?...........34
11. What is Recovery Really? 36
12. Recovery - It's Up To You 38
13. How Do I Know If I Am Recovering? 40
14. Revenge 42
15. Can I Really Forgive? 44
16. Master Your Rage 46
17. Expectations 48
18. What is Love? 50
19. Spiritual Rejuvenation 52
20. Does God Hear My Prayers? 54
21. Do You Like Being The Victim? 56

22. Morning Blues? 58

23. There is Hope 60

24. How Do I Release My Hurt? 62

25. Realize That God Is Always With You 64

26. The Pain Lasts Longer Than Expected 66

27. Lost Cause? 68

28. Showing Compassion 70

29. Being Unable to Function 72

30. Where Does Your Help Come From? 74

31. Losing Identity 76

32. The Joy Does Return 78

33. Finding Comfort 80

34. Starting the Healing Journey 82

35. Don't Push It Down 84

36. Finding Your Way 86

37. Are You In A Hurry? 88

38. Are Other's Helping or Hurting? 90

39. Roller Coaster Ride 92

40. The Black Hole 94

41. Time 96

42. Hour By Hour 98

43. Holidays 100

44. Mourning Your Marriage 102

45. Being In Control 104

46. Society's Response to Grief 106

47. Hiding 108

48. Faith Brings Joy 110

49. Seeking Help 112

50. Give Up or Go On 114

51. Do You Trust Him? 116

52. Anger: Slow and Steady 118

53. Anger: Is It Wrong? 120

54. Anger: Losing Control of Life 122

55. Anger: Be Honest With How You Feel 124

56. Angry with God 126

57. Anger: Source and Limits 128

58. Anger: Unchecked Can Lead To Bitterness .. 130

59. Anger: Moving On 132

60. Blame 134

61. Bitterness and Resentment 136

62. Bitterness and Depression 138

63. Regrets 140

64. Depression 142

65. Depression: Two Kinds of Losses 144

66. Depression: Devise a Plan 146

67. Depression: Stop Your Negative Thoughts 148

68. Depression: Get Rid of False Beliefs 150

69. Depression: Be Willing to Set Limits 152

70. Depression: Yes, There Is an End 154

71. Unresolved Emotions and Isolation 156

72. How Are You Feeling? 158

73. Satan is Attacking 160

74. Forgiveness 162

75. Forgiveness: It's Your Choice 164

76. Forgiveness: The Catalyst to Healing 166

77. Forgiving the Other Person 168

78. Forgiveness Will Set You Free 170

79. Forgiving Yourself 172

80. One Step Forward, Two Steps Back 174

81. Destructive Choices 176

82. Self-Esteem 178

83. Trust 180

84. Moving Past the "Whys" 182

85. Personal Boundaries 184

86. Telling the Children 186

87. What if the Children Already Know? 188

88. God's Will in Your Life 190

89. Do You Have An Active Prayer Life? 192

90. The Only Healing Relationship 194

Introduction

I was a stay at home homeschooling mom of two boys; aged 7 and 8, and had been married for 12 years to a great guy. At the time I thought I had it all, great kids, a place of our own, our own business, and money in the bank. I was happy and I thought my husband was too. I mean, sure, we had our problems just like everyone else but I truly thought we were okay.

Things started to crack when I started hearing rumors that my husband was seeing another woman. I have always believed that my husband would never have an affair. I would have bet any amount of money that he would never be caught up in an affair. I just could never fathom him stepping out on me.

When people would tell me that he was seeing someone else I would ask him about it and he would always deny it. He was so good at lying that I believed him, or maybe I just so badly didn't want it to be true that I believed him. Somehow, I would gloss it all over like everything was just fine, put my rose colored glasses back on and pretend things were fine.

Then one day in July, my mom came to me saying the same things others had been saying. Now, she doesn't even live here, she lives 500 miles away, but she came up to visit for a week. Finally, something in me snapped and I had had enough. I tracked my husband down and told him we had to talk and to meet me down by the lake.

This time I didn't ask, "Are you having an affair?" because I never got the truth with that. This time I asked, "Do you want a divorce?" He said, "No, why?" I then said, "Because you're seeing someone else." He didn't say a word and I knew then it was true. I then asked, "How long?" He replied, "A year." That afternoon he told me everything and answered any question I had.

Reality as I knew it disappeared. To say I was shocked would be an understatement. I was beyond hurt. I really didn't believe I could go on. The pain was excruciating. I felt like all my insides liquefied and drained right out of me. I literally couldn't feel my body. I sat there listening to him with my mind and body totally numb. This is God's way of getting us through moments like this, it's called shock. One thought I did have during this time is, "Don't make any rash decisions." I am glad I didn't either because at this moment all I could see is pain, devastation, darkness and complete hopelessness.

My marriage and dreams crumbled at my feet. My heart shattered into a million pieces as the world fell out from under me. I had no idea how I would ever put my life back together again. At that moment, I felt I would never feel happiness again. That was July 21st, 2004.

I spent the next two years looking for a way to make the pain go away. I read every book I could get my hands on. I went to counselors and marriage coaches. Nothing seemed to work for me. I was still full of pain, anger and bitterness after two years of trying.

It was then that I decided to start attending church. As my spiritual soul was being fed, I looked for a devotional specifically for the betrayed spouse. Much to my amazement, I came up empty. There are devotionals for nearly any topic you can think of, but there were none for healing after infidelity. This was very surprising to me as infidelity touches over 60% of all marriages.

For two years, I would hear inside my heart, "Why don't you write a devotional for those hurting over affairs?" I would then in turn reply, "I can't do that, I'm not a writer. Who would want to read anything I have to say?" This continued for almost a year until I finally threw up my hands and said, "Okay, Okay, I'll write one!" And now, I am very glad I did.

Giving my pain, fears, heartache and emotions over to God is what started my true healing journey. The steps were never easy and the results were never instant but the healing did come. You just need to learn to grab a hold of God's promises, one at a time, and take baby steps forward toward healing. This will not be a magical journey and your situation isn't just going to disappear overnight. But you will see a shift in your attitude and that is the beginning of making a huge difference.

If you are in the same pain that I was once in, I empathize with you with my entire heart. Please know that you are not alone. I have a very deep desire to help those who are suffering in pain and agony because of their spouse's affair. I want to reach out and just hug them. I want to tell them that it can, and will, get better and to just hold on and take it one small step at a time.

I want you to know that my husband and I didn't have smooth sailing into healing and recovery. We had to work hard and process all our thoughts and emotions. It was not easy and at times was extremely raw and messy. We were both surprised at how long this recovery road really was. But if you ask either of us if it was worth all the pain, heartache and hard work we would both give a resounding yes!

My desire to help led me to not only write this devotional, but to become certified in relationship coaching and grief recovery. Many people suffer in silence because infidelity is almost always kept quiet and hush-hush. This is especially true in a church community. I want to give those that are hurting a sense of hope and a road map to healing.

My hope and prayer is for you to use the devotional and the accompanying **_Godly Whispers Workbook_** to help guide you out of the darkness and pain and into God's shinning light of hope. I want you to know that hope is real and will be a reality in your life regardless of what your spouse has done or may still be doing. There is always hope for anyone that seeks out God. I have watched people struggle through the hard and often messy work that resulted in their full healing.

I have been where you are, caught in the depths of an unimaginable pain and lost in the horrifying darkness. But you will find, just as I did, that no matter how deep your pain runs, God runs deeper! God's peace and healing are there for anyone who wants and needs them. You also can experience His healing hand as He makes you whole again. You will discover that there is hope and complete healing after infidelity.

Don't view the word "hope" as being a dream or wishful thinking. God's definition of the word "hope" is

Promise. Hope is a firm promise about the things that are unclear and unknown to us. Like all of God's promises, it's a certainty; there are no ifs, ands or buts about it! You will find, like I did, that God's promises are your security and certainty during this time in your life. He alone is our hope while we heal after our spouse's infidelity.

If you want to know what God's direction for your life is, the best place to start is in His Word. That is why I made the **_Godly Whispers Workbook_** to go along with this devotional. This workbook will give you extra bible verses to read that go along with every devotion so that you can get deeper into His Word every day. Some of the verses you may already know, but God will reveal new things to you which you have never seen before even if you have read those verses many times prior.

I also want these devotions to be a journey of self-discovery and that is another reason why I made the workbook to go along with this devotional book. Every day, besides the extra bible verses, there are deep and thought provoking questions that will help you delve deeper into yourself and help you process all your thoughts and feelings. To process your thoughts and feelings is to deeply think about each of them and then to explore them in all honesty.

I have always strongly suggested to those I work with that they keep a daily journal daily. By keeping your own it will help you get your thoughts out of your head to make space for better things. There are 2 full pages for you to journal on every day in the **_Godly Whispers Workbook_**. Everything is right there for you all in one book. You may hate the idea of journaling or maybe you believe that you just hate writing. I also felt this way when I first started doing it, but someone made me do it anyway and now I am glad I did. No matter how much you don't want to, do it anyway! You can begin by writing down any thoughts you have as you read the devotional and your bible. I give you thought provoking questions to help sort out your emotions so that you can journal more easily.

I do want to warn you that some of truths found in this devotional you will want to run from and pretend they do not exist. With every fiber of your being you will want to resist the change that needs to be made to move forward. When this happens, please don't hesitate to repeat the devotion again the next day and even the next day until you can completely apply the change in your life. Again, this is where the journaling comes in. Write down all your feelings about not wanting to do something or why you don't want to do it. Even if you are angry, write those feelings out. These feelings are not wrong! Bring them to God, He will listen. Work through these new ideas and beliefs through prayer and journaling.

Through your daily journaling I want you to process all your thoughts and feelings no matter how ugly they are. Don't bother trying to write all nicey, nice as God already sees and knows your whole heart. He already knows everything that is in there so you aren't going to surprise Him with anything and what may surprise you is that He still loves you just as much as He always did.

Even if you are a new Christian or have been following God for years, expect Him to reveal Himself and His promises to you as you read this devotional and His Word. Always remember that God as not abandoned you! Right now, He is calling out to you to come find comfort in

His loving arms. You will find that God is more than able to lead you down the right path. He will teach you through your pain. You will find that as you seek him more and more each day His loving encouragement will continue day after day.

When I decided to use devotionals and read His Word every day, I started to feel God's intimate touch in a much new and more powerful way than ever before. I felt like God was taking care of my specific needs with His loving words of truth. I could actually see evidence of His work and loving care in my life. This new habit of reading a devotional and my bible became my lifeline. The verses seemed to be written just for me like **Genesis 22:14** in which is simply states "the Lord will provide". God wants to work through you and in you, no matter what your spouse does or does not do. Decide who you are going to follow and whose voice you will listen to.

Are you feeling alone in your pain? I don't believe any betrayed spouse should ever feel that they need to suffer alone in their pain, with no one there for them to turn to. There is no need for you to keep your pain a secret. If you need someone to talk to right away, please feel free to email me and I will help you any way I can.

If there are other devotions you would love to see around the subject of infidelity please email me and let me know what they are, I wouldn't mind writing another devotional book.

marsharozalski@godlywhispers.com
www.godlywhispers.com

Bible References

NIV - New International Version
NLT - New Living Translation
NASB - New American Standard Bible
EBV - American Standard Version
TLB - The Living Bible

1

When Your World Has Ended

"For I know the plans I have for you," declares the LORD, "plans to prosper you and not to harm you, plans to give you hope and a future."
Jeremiah 29:11 (NIV)

Discovering your spouse has been unfaithful is the most devastating experience anyone could ever go through. It's a day when the world no longer makes sense. You're likely to experience every emotion from feeling empty to abandoned, betrayed to shamed, angered to depressed. You may feel many of these intense emotions so deeply and rapidly that you may sometimes feel you just can't go on. Your self-esteem is damaged, and you may be wondering how you are going to survive the next few months when you can't even make it through today.

Regardless of how you *feel*, be assured that God is always with you. He said in **Hebrews 13:5**, *"I will never leave you, nor forsake you."* If ever there was a time to pray, today is the day. He alone is our Master Healer, a God of reconciliation and a mender of broken hearts and shattered lives. God wants to take your pain, and turn it into a message of hope. He can turn our trials into something life changing if we just let Him.

We all have experienced devastations and crises in our lives. When we find ourselves in these situations, we must learn not give up hope. We must do our part and continue living and being productive. God does have a plan for us but His plan might not be on our timing. You may want to be better right now, but this may not be in His plan. As long as we keep our eyes on Him and listen to His wisdom then we know we are heading in the right direction. He only wants what is best for you, always remember that.

We must learn to come to him in prayer for when we do, He will always listen. We must seek Him with our full heart giving our full selves to Him. Then, and only then, will we find Him. He will bring us out of our deep sorrow so that we can experience His will in our lives. God wants us to live a happy and abundant life here on earth and He can give that to us. His true will for our lives will be realized when we meet Him in prayer and meditation.

Today's Prayer

Dear Lord,

Thank You for having a wonderful plan for my life. I know and trust that You will never leave me, or forsake me. I lay my future in Your hands knowing that you have my best interest at heart. Lord, You alone are the only One that can heal my broken heart and mend my shattered soul. Please wrap Your loving arms around me, and let me lean on You in my darkest hour. Thank You for being the wonderful God that You are. Amen.

2

Shock

"We've been surrounded and battered by troubles, but we're not demoralized; we're not sure what to do, but we know that God knows what to do; we've been spiritually terrorized, but God hasn't left our side; we've been thrown down, but we haven't broken."
2 Corinthians 4:8-9 (NIV)

The moment I found out that my husband had been having an affair over the past year, I was floored. It was a total shock to my system. I went into a state of crisis. I was extremely overwhelmed and slammed with so many emotions that I shut down. It stopped me in my tracks, with no idea of which way to go next. For the next 24 hours, I literally could not think straight and it felt like I was on another planet. I have never experienced that kind of pain before and I literally thought I was dying.

Shock is defined as the feeling of distress and disbelief that you have when something horrible happens. I'm sure you, also, had this paralyzing reaction. You realize that you are no longer in control of your world, and that the world as you have known it, is no longer real. When you're in a state of shock, feeling unable to cope or even think straight, know that you don't have to survive this alone. God is right there holding open His arms for you to fly into.

Because of all the turmoil that is going on inside you, it is not wise to make any major changes or decisions in your life. When you make decisions based on your emotions, almost always, they are later much regretted. Never decide on important issues until you are able to get your emotions under control, no matter how long that takes. So, unless you are in mediate danger, don't just run out and file for divorce. If you need the space away from your spouse for a while then do so. Just don't make any life changing decisions before you have had time to process all your emotions.

During this time in your life the Lord will always remain at your side and He will keep you from being totally destroyed. You need to claim the promises in His Word as your own no matter how you are feeling or what is happening in your life right now. You need to cling to God with everything you have. He will guard your life and give you comfort. Always remember that God's strength will see you through this, all you have to do is place your trust in Him.

Today's Prayer

Dear Lord,

Oh Lord, I'm in such pain I feel totally crushed and broken. I am utterly confused and overwhelmed, but I refuse to give up hope. I feel I have been spiritually terrorized. I am so thankful that You have not left my side. I am putting my trust in You. I know You know what to do, and I will follow where you lead me. Thank You for being the wonderful God that You are. Amen

3

Why Lord?

"Don't worry about anything; instead, pray about
everything. Tell God what you need, and thank him for all
he has done. Then you will experience God's peace,
which exceeds anything we can understand. His peace
will guard your hearts and minds as you live in Christ
Jesus."
Philippians 4:6-7 (NLT)

This question haunted me longer than I want to admit. This question can be absolutely devastating, because often there isn't any answer. Even though you yearn to know the answer to "why", you must learn to refuse to lean on your own understanding. It's not for us to understand the why, but to put our faith and trust in God knowing that He has our best interest at heart. We may feel that God has left us and that we have to deal with this pain alone, but that is not true. We know He has a plan for us, and even though we don't understand why this is happening, we do know God has promised that His peace will guard our hearts and minds as we live in Him.

Don't mistake this peace. This does not mean that life will be easy and no harm will come to you. It's more of an inner peace that has no explanation, because we possess it when everyone says we shouldn't. This peace is a gift from God, not a result of anything we do or don't do. This peace is our comfort in Christ. God is so in love with you and He wants only the best for you. All you need to do is pray and obey His Word. This peace will be there even when you are experiencing hard times. You will find that you have an inner peace about things and that even though things are hard you will know that you'll be okay because of your faith in God.

This peace is the "peace of God," bestowed upon us by His grace. Grace is defined in the Word of God as something that will teach you how to live. (**Titus 2:11-12**) Please don't throw away this peace that God is offering you. Immerse yourself in His Word, meditate on the verses that bring you the most comfort and in doing so, you will see that inner peace is much easier to find.

Today's Prayer

Dear Lord,

I am so thankful that I can depend on You when I feel so lost and alone. Lord, teach me to rest in Your love for me, and trust in Your wisdom and power. Help me to feed my heart and my soul with things that nurture my trust in You. Lord, teach me how to no longer lean on my own understanding but to trust fully in You knowing that You will show me which way I am to go. Thank You for the wonderful peace that You have bestowed upon me today. Thank You for being the wonderful God that You are. Amen.

4

The Level of Pain

"In all their suffering he (Jesus) also suffered, and he
personally rescued them. In his love and mercy he
redeemed them. He lifted them up and carried them
through all the years."
Isaiah 63:9 (NLT)

❧

     I felt like there was no way that I could survive the level of pain I was feeling. I just knew that you couldn't have this kind of pain and live. This was the most excruciating pain I had ever experienced in all my life. I kept thinking that I was truly going to die, but amazingly, I never did. I remember asking God to just take me now because dying seemed so much better than living. A lot of those suffering from the pain of a spouse's affair have suicidal thoughts. This is very normal because of the amount of pain they are in. Seek help if these thoughts last longer than two weeks or you are planning to carry the thoughts out.

     The level of pain you are in is beyond anyone else's comprehension unless they too have experienced their own spouse's infidelity. Others around you will mean well, but there is no way they can ever understand how deep your pain runs and why it would have such a severe effect on the emotional, mental, physical and spiritual aspects of your life. Your spouse will never *really* understand the depths of your emotions. I pray they will try hard to understand, empathize and really get what you are going through.   When this happens healing becomes much easier.

Anxiety, sadness, devastation and pain are all associated with infidelity and they are all thieves.   They rob you and your whole family of things like time and the ability to just enjoy the day.   It's so hard to live in the present when you're suffering from trauma and extreme negative thinking.   The faster you can get through all these emotional hurdles, the better.

It's also wonderful to know that no matter how deep your pain runs, God truly feels the level of your pain. You might think that God really doesn't care.   Maybe your pain has caused your heart to turn hard against God, but He really does understand physical suffering.   He truly does understand your pain and He wants to comfort you in your suffering. All you need to do is call out to Him and He will come to you and help ease your pain.

Today's Prayer

Dear Lord,

Only You know how deep my pain runs.   Please rescue me from this horrible pain and send me Your peace and comfort.   Please carry me in Your arms because I am in too much pain to continue on my own. Thank You for loving me enough to save me from this awful pain. Thank You for being the wonderful God that You are. Amen.

5

Call Upon a Friend

*"All praise to God, the Father of our Lord Jesus Christ.
God is our merciful Father and the source of all comfort.
He comforts us in all our troubles so that we can comfort
others. When they are troubled, we will be able to give
them the same comfort God has given us."*
2 Corinthians 1:3-4 (NLT)

Don't go through this alone. I see so many that refuse to tell anyone and they are left to suffer in their pain alone. One of the smartest things I did was call a friend to share my heartbreak with. Sometimes we don't want to call anyone because we are embarrassed about the situation, or we don't want our friends and family to have hard feelings toward our spouse. Just be certain that the person you entrust isn't going to spread the news all over town. Be sure it's someone you completely trust and that they have your best interests at heart.

The troubles mentioned in the above verses are referring to things that consume your mind continually and endanger your well-being, refusing to leave you alone. It depresses you and causes you to view your future with dark forebodings of miserable unhappiness. Have you had the opportunity to help others when they have been faced with hard times? It feels good to help others, doesn't it? If we don't call on our friends and family during our time of need, we deprive them of that blessing. Jesus said, *"It is more blessed to give than to receive."* –

Acts 20:35. If our pride gets in the way of asking for support, we rob those who know us of a blessing. One day they will come to find out about our adversity and will feel hurt that we didn't turn to them in our time of need.

Isn't it comforting to know that our hardships aren't in vain, that God has a purpose for them, not only for us but for others as well? Our hardships bring us closer to God and to each other as we look for comfort and seek to give it as well. Comfort is a lot more than a bit of cheer or a word of encouragement. The word comfort means "to strengthen" and God wants to be your comfort and strength. God is always there for us when we are going through a hard time, and before you know it He brings someone else who is going through the same hard time we are so we can be there for each other just as God was there for us.

Today's Prayer

Dear Lord,

Thank You Lord that even in this ordeal there is something positive that I can grab hold of. Thank You that one day I can comfort someone who will go through what I have been through. And thank You that there are those who can comfort me through my current storms. Help me to open my heart to the comfort of others and to find others who can relate to what I am enduring. Thank You for being the wonderful God that You are. Amen.

6

Let the Church Help You

"And let us not neglect our meeting together, as some people do, but encourage one another, especially now that the day of his return is drawing near."
Hebrews 10:25 (NLT)

God has always intended for the church to provide support and loving hearts to help others who are hurting and in need. The energy, and the solid foundation, of the church is Jesus Christ. He loves you unconditionally. Even if you feel like you have to hide your "terrible secret", help is still there for you.

You don't need to tell everyone, but you need to find one or two people within the church you can really trust. This way you will have people praying for you and with you. If you are not close with anyone in your church or you don't have a home church, please search around for one that you are comfortable in. Pray that God will lead you to the right church and the right people.

The worst thing during this time would be to withdraw from other Christians. Right now you need them more than any other time in your life. You need their encouragement, prayers and support. They can help keep your focus on God instead of on your problems. I found one woman that really helped me and prayed for me all the time. She made a wonderful difference in my life and she was a true blessing to me. God will bring someone into your life that will be such a blessing to you, all you need to do is ask. Caring people can make all the difference in the world when it comes to your healing.

God has promised in His Word that He will take care of all your needs. It can be any kind of need— emotional, physical or spiritual. He will use the people in your church to help you on your healing journey. All you need to do is ask. Pray that God will send you the right people that you need in your life right now. Don't give up; God will answer your prayers. Have faith that God will do as He promises in His Word. Claim those promises as your own and pray them back to Him and thank Him in advance for what He will do for you.

Today's Prayer

Dear Lord,

Help me to find the right people in my church to help me along this hard road and to pray for me during this difficult time. Please open my heart to find and accept the love and help of those in my church. Help me to not shy away from those that might be trying to reach out to me. Thank You for being the wonderful God that You are. Amen.

7

You Need Friends

"Two people are better off than one, for they can help each other succeed. If one person falls, the other can reach out and help. But someone who falls alone is in real trouble."
Ecclesiastes 4:9-10 (NLT)

You need to get yourself emotionally stabilized. Even though this can be very difficult, it's an important part of your healing. Did you know that about 85% of all your energy is being used up by your intense emotions? Literally, I could sit on the couch all day, but still be totally exhausted in just a few hours. My mind was racing with thoughts of the affair, and my emotions were all over the map.

When dealing with a spouse's affair, it's very easy to become emotionally drained in a very short period of time. Being slammed with so many kinds of emotions in a short period of time can cause an adrenaline rush which increases your heart rate causing your body to become exhausted.

One way to stabilize your emotions is to have same-sex friendships. Do NOT become friends with someone of the opposite sex, because this can lead you down the road to an affair and make matters much worse. Same-sex friends will provide you with emotional stability. They can keep you from making poor choices and help build you up. They can show you what's good about yourself and help you grow to be all that God wants you to be. They are there for you to lean on and to offer you comfort when you are hurting. Right now you may be feeling very unloved and they will shower you will the love you so badly need. You will also not feel so alone when you have someone there to share all your feelings with.

Make sure these friends share your same faith so that you may pray together and they can help you grow in the Lord. Have them pray for you and with you. They can be there for you when the pain becomes too much to bare. If you don't have anyone like this right now, pray that the Lord will bring someone into your life. Always remember that God wants to be your best friend. You can always go to Him any time and tell Him anything. He will never forsake you, put you down or make you feel unloved.

Today's Prayer

Dear Lord,

Please help me find a good Christian friend that I can lean on. Please give me the motivation to call upon someone, to get together and talk, and to build a close friendship with. Thank You for being the wonderful God that You are. Amen.

8

Where is God?

"For He [God] Himself has said, I will not in any way fail you nor give you up nor leave you without support. [I will] not, [I will] not, [I will] not in any degree leave you helpless nor forsake nor let [you] down (relax My hold on you)! [Assuredly not!]"
Hebrews 13:5 (Amplified Bible)

The profound fear behind our loss is that God, who we thought should have saved us, has abandoned us. You may feel that, if He hadn't forsaken you, this would have never happened to you, your family and your marriage. You may ask yourself, "Where is God and why did He let this happen?" But I'm here to tell you that God has never left you. God promised you that He will never leave, forsake or abandon you. He will be with you forever through everything you will ever experience. God is the same yesterday, today and forever.

Nothing can separate us from the love of God. God will never break His promises to us and we must learn to put our faith into His promises. Learn to focus on His promises and to keep them close to your heart. Find ones that mean the most to you and memorize them so you can meditate on them during the day.

The difference we have as Christians is that even though we grieve, we can grieve in the hope of the Lord. You have to make up your mind, are you going to believe in the Word of God or in your circumstances? God has a wonderful plan for your life and He wants nothing more than to see you happy.

When your thoughts are telling you that God has abandoned you, you must tell yourself that these are just lies being whispered to you by Satan. The conflict of faith is in the mind. Our thoughts can cause us the most grief. You'll find that once a negative thought enters your mind that it's so easy to keep them coming. The next thing you know, it is hours later and you're either deeply depressed or very angry. Every moment we must choose whose thoughts we are going to listen to, our own or God's. Whose thoughts contain the most truth?

Today's Prayer

Dear Lord,

Please help me in my time of pain and loss. I don't understand why my life is filled with this pain and heartache. Lord, teach me to turn to You to find the strength to trust in Your faithfulness. My heart is crushed, but I know that You will not abandon me. Please show me Your compassion, Lord. Help me through the pain and help me to hope in You again. Though I can't see past today, I trust Your great love will never fail me. Thank You for being the wonderful God that You are. Amen

9

Overwhelmed?

"O God, listen to my cry! Hear my prayer! From the ends of the earth, I cry to you for help when my heart is overwhelmed. Lead me to the towering rock of safety, for you are my safe refuge, a fortress where my enemies cannot reach me. Let me live forever in your sanctuary, safe beneath the shelter of your wings!"
Psalms 61:1-4 (NLT)

Knowing that your spouse has had an affair is extremely overwhelming. For the first month I could barely function. I couldn't do the normal every day things that needed done. I couldn't seem to focus on anything except the affair. The affair seemed to be an all-consuming thought in my mind. It seemed to have taken over my whole body. To say that life at this time was overwhelming would be an understatement. You need to understand that you are not alone and your problem is not unique.

You need to cry out to the Lord when you feel overwhelmed because our relief comes from Him. The secret in finding relief is to fully trust the Lord, because He knows and understands our pain. Don't avoid your pain by finding other outlets. Don't push your pain down hoping it will just go away over time. Take your pain to the Lord. Only in our pain do we grow and learn to lean on Him. Our goal should be to grow in our relationship with the Lord.   Our anguish becomes the catalyst of our growth.

If you are feeling overwhelmed, you have let your heart and mind drift from God.   You must anchor your attention on the Lord rather than the affair. If you divert your focus away from the affair and onto Him, the Lord will reward your faith and give you His perfect peace. **Isaiah 26:3 (NLT)** *"You will keep in perfect peace all who trust in you, all whose thoughts are fixed on you!"*

God knows your pain.   Don't think that He doesn't know every thought and every feeling you have.   Don't be ashamed or afraid to bring them to Him.   Only He can bring you the peace you so desperately long for. You need to start praising and thanking Him for His love and care for you. When you worship God it brings you closer to Him and you will experience His most amazing love and peace.

Today's Prayer

Dear Lord,

I need You today because I am overwhelmed. Reading Your Word brings me comfort. I ask You to come and take my heavy burdens. Please carry them for me so I don't have to. Replace them with an inner peace so that I will find rest for my soul today. Thank You for the perfect peace that You have bestowed upon me today. Thank You for being the wonderful God that You are. Amen.

10

Is This Really Happening?

*"Get the truth and never sell it; also get wisdom,
discipline, and good judgment."*
Proverbs 23:23 (NLT)

*"Happy (blessed, fortunate, enviable) is the man who
finds skillful and godly Wisdom, and the man who gets
understanding [drawing it forth from God's Word and life's
experiences]"*
Proverbs 3:13 (Amplified Bible)

Just about everyone experiences shock after first finding out about the affair. I was in a state of shock for quite a while after I first found out. This time period is different for everyone. It might be a long time or a short time for you. During this time you may experience a lot of denial. You may feel like your whole marriage was a big lie, or at least the part of it that was during the affair. Nothing may feel real to you. This is a defense mechanism that your mind and body uses to reduce the pain. It is a natural part of the healing journey.

You will find yourself asking if this is really happening. You will find that your mind knows the facts while your heart just can't accept any of it. You may even find yourself diving into something just to fill your mind with anything but the truth about what is going on in your marriage. Distraction may work for a short while, but it won't last. When denial stops working, you will be faced with the truth of it all. You must always be open to the truth and go after it. Never run from the truth because the truth will set you free. Knowing the truth and finding the answers to your questions will empower you. This is why it's important to have all your questions answered honestly by your spouse. By knowing the true answers to all your questions you will find it much easier to heal.

Building a relationship with God will help you face the truth. Sometimes the truth will cause you great pain, but with God by your side, you can overcome the powerful sorrow, because God is stronger than our pain. The more you pray and seek God's Word, the easier it will be for you to accept and heal from the things that have happened in your marriage. It's not going to be easy, and it's not going to be fast, but you will survive with God on your side.

Today's Prayer

Dear Lord,

I need You to send me the courage I will need to face the truth about the affair, and my marriage. It's not something I can do alone, but I know I need to do it. I know that with Your help I can face whatever lies ahead. Thank You for being the wonderful God that You are. Amen.

11

What is Recovery Really?

*"But He was wounded for our transgressions, He was
bruised for our guilt and iniquities; the chastisement
[needful to obtain] peace and well-being for us was upon
Him, and with the stripes [that wounded] Him we are
healed and made whole."*
Isaiah 53:5 (Amplified Bible)

Until my husband had his affair, I really had no
idea what recovery was all about. I get asked all the time
how long recovery takes, and at what stage of recovery
should someone be at any given time. The recovery
process is so different for every couple. There are many
different levels of recovery. Two separate people, six
months out from finding out about the affair will very likely
be in two totally different places in their recovery.

You know you are recovering when you are aware
of what you have lost and that you never want to go
through that kind of pain again. Recovery is also moving
forward and this is usually very painful and slow. You
have to accept what has happened as truth. Understand
that, yes, this really did happen. You must then go
through the painful process of grieving. For everyone, the
time line is different but until you decide that you want to
recover, the healing journey will not begin.

Some who find out about their spouse's affair
never really heal. They hang on to the hurt and pain,

which then turn into bitterness and hatred. They would rather hang onto being right and/or being a victim than forgiving and learning to love again. I have seen those that are still very angry and bitter about their spouse's affair that happened over 20 years ago, even though they have remained married. I knew I never wanted to be like that, because for me, that is no way to live.

Recovery is turning back to God. He is the Master Healer and He wants to set you free from your pain. He will give you a new life in Him. This is the only real way to recover. I don't believe there is any other way to fully and completely recover. Recovery can only be complete through Jesus Christ. Receiving God's restoration and comfort starts with you turning to Him and laying all your hurt and pain at His feet. You need to empty your whole heart to Him so He can start the healing your broken heart.

Today's Prayer

Dear Lord,

Thank You for the giving of Yourself so that I may be healed and made whole again. Please help me to keep moving forward towards healing. It's a long hard road and I know the only way I am going to be completely healed is through You. Please help me not to hang on to any bitterness or hatred towards my spouse. Thank You for being the wonderful God that You are. Amen.

12

Recovery - It's Up To You

"So then, since Christ suffered physical pain, you must arm yourselves with the same attitude he had, and be ready to suffer, too. For if you have suffered physically for Christ, you have finished with sin. You won't spend the rest of your lives chasing your own desires, but you will be anxious to do the will of God."
1 Peter 4:1-2 (NLT)

You have a lot of choices when it comes to your recovery. Hopefully you will make the right choices. I am sad to say that some of my choices were not the right ones and this caused my recovery to become much longer and drawn out. We all didn't have the choice whether or not we went through this devastation, but we do have other choices we can make and one of those is our attitude.

A big component in recovery is attitude. You can choose what kind of attitude to have towards the events that unfold in your life. You can either choose to have an attitude of bitterness and hatred, which will make your life miserable and deteriorate your health. Or you can have an attitude of willingness—willingness to work through all your feelings—to learn from them and become a better person.

Which one are you going to choose? Do you want to live the rest of your life with bitterness and hatred, or do you want to work through your feelings and problems and learn from them? The choice is up to you.

I realized that I didn't like the person I was becoming. Bitterness and hatred where becoming the norm, and I didn't like myself very much anymore. I knew that because of my attitude we would end up divorced if I didn't change. It took me 2 years to figure this out. Please, don't be like I was. Choose to work through your feelings and move forward towards healing. You will come out on the other side a much better person because of it.

It's comforting to know that Jesus knows all about suffering as He suffered enormously while He was here on earth. But did you know that He always chose the attitude of seeing it through because He knew the benefits of moving forward through the pain. You need to focus on where you want your life to be, not where it is or has been. Then work on repairing your life and marriage the way that God instructs you to.

Today's Prayer

Dear Lord,

Please help me work through my pain and hurt and give me an attitude of wanting to work through our problems. Help me to be a better person for it. Please help me choose more positive thoughts and actions in my marriage and my life. Thank You for being the wonderful God that You are. Amen.

13

How Do I Know If I Am Recovering?

"The young women will dance for joy, and the men—old and young—will join in the celebration. I will turn their mourning into joy. I will comfort them and exchange their sorrow for rejoicing."
Jeremiah 31:13 (NLT)

ᕦᏛᕤ

You would be surprised at how many people ask me this question. I used to ask it myself. I couldn't wait for the day I could finally say, "I have recovered." I used to believe it was all about time. I remember hearing that infidelity takes 2-5 years to recover from. So, I couldn't wait till the 2-year mark came, because then I would be "all better". I was devastated when it came and I wasn't much better. Recovery isn't ONLY about time, but what you DO in that time.

So, how do you know that you are recovering? You'll know because you'll no longer feel anger, bitterness, blame, resentment or self-pity. Recovery means that you feel better. Another great sign that you are recovering is that you think about the affair less and less often. Also, when you do there is less and less pain associated with it. If you are living in the here and now more than you are obsessing with the past, you are recovering. When you start having more good days than bad, you know you are recovering.

4 months out from D-Day I wondered if I was ever going to think about anything else besides the affair. It had consumed me and I really wanted it to stop, but those thoughts seemed to have a life of their own. Then one day I realized I had gone hours without thinking about it, and I was amazed. I really could think about something else! I also began noticing that I was having more good days in a row than before. It was a painfully slow process, but it did happen. One day you will also find that you will think about the affair less often. Also, you'll have more good days than bad.

Another indicator that you're recovering is when you can feel the peace of Christ within you. Recovery doesn't mean that the pain is now gone. You will still have painful triggers that come out of nowhere for several years. Know that this is normal, and be ready to conquer them with things like prayer, positive and uplifting scriptures, and positive reaffirming statements. The Lord will turn your mourning into joy if you let Him work in your heart.

Today's Prayer

Dear Lord,

Thank You for all the signs of recovery in my life. Thank You for always being there for me when I am experiencing a painful trigger. Please help me to stay moving forward on this road of recovery. Please help me to see all the positive things in my life and marriage. Thank You for being the wonderful God that You are. Amen.

14

Revenge

"Do not take revenge, my friends, but leave room for God's wrath, for it is written: "It is mine to avenge; I will repay," says the Lord."
Romans 12:19 (NIV)

Are you thinking about "getting even" and having an affair yourself? I want you to know this is very natural to want to get back at your spouse for cheating on you. I had those same feelings too. I actually wanted to go out and "have fun" just like he did. If he could, so could I right? A revenge affair never has the desired results you want and it will most likely backfire in many ways. I have seen many marriages fall apart because the betrayed spouse went out and had an affair too.

A revenge affair won't ever solve the problem or make you hurt any less. In fact, it can have the exact opposite effect. Instead of solving the situation with your spouse, you destroy what is left of your marriage. This is why I strongly discourage revenge affairs whenever I talk with infidelity victims. In hind sight, I am so glad I never went through with my thoughts of having a revenge affair.

I'm sure you've heard these sayings; tit for tat, an eye for an eye, a tooth for a tooth, don't get mad, get even and fight fire with fire. Have you ever sought revenge only to be unfulfilled with the end result? When you take revenge against someone else you don't get that satisfied feeling of justice you are looking for. Please don't seek revenge on others, let God take care of the vengeance. The Lord is going to take care of you, so don't worry about "getting even." He is the only one who can make it right and the only one whose justice can truly work.

We don't need to seek revenge because God is the only one who weighs man's actions. He gives them just as they deserve – in His perfect timing. The Word states that God really does take revenge, but it will only come from His all-knowing and just hands. You must have faith that God truly sees your situation. You must believe that God rewards good behavior and punishes bad behavior. It's a promise found in His Word. Look up **Galatians 6:7** and **Luke 14:13-14.**

Today's Prayer

Dear Lord,

Sometimes the urge to take revenge is so strong; please guard my heart against these thoughts. Please remove the bitterness I have towards my spouse. I surrender all my feelings of revenge to You. Forgive me and help me change my attitude. Lord, I believe in You and I love You above all things. Thank You for being the wonderful God that You are. Amen.

15

Can I Really Forgive?

"Pay attention and always be on your guard [looking out for one another]. If your brother sins (misses the mark), solemnly tell him so and reprove him, and if he repents (feels sorry for having sinned), forgive him."
Luke 17:3 (Amplified Bible)

This may be the hardest thing to you'll ever do, to forgive your spouse for betraying you and your marriage. In fact, you might not be able to fathom it right now, and that is okay. I had to work on forgiveness every day. Forgiveness is not a feeling but a process and it won't happen overnight but it should be something you're always moving towards. Forgiveness is rarely a one-time occurrence. You work on it one day at a time and one decision at a time. We can also learn to say, "I forgive you" every day until one day we realize that we really do mean it.

Is your spouse truly sorry? Do they have true remorse for the wrong they have done to you? Do you believe they "get" what they have done to you? According to scripture we are to forgive those that truly repent for the wrong they have done. Nobody said this was going to be easy but through God it can be done. You don't have to take my word for it, pray and work with God and find out for yourself what it feels like to truly forgive your spouse.

Forgiveness is more a gift you give yourself. You don't forgive to make yourself look good or to change the other person. Harboring unforgiveness only hurts you-not the other person. It's like drinking poison and expecting the other person to die. You will find that true forgiveness brings peace back into your life. Granting your forgiveness isn't saying that you approve of or condone their behavior but rather you're handing it over to God and asking Him to deal with it according to His will.

You must remember that God knows the wrong that was done. He knows how deeply your pain runs. If you can just go to Him, willing to forgive your spouse through God's power, you will be able to move forward in your healing. You will then be able to lay all your pain and anguish in His hands. God can and will change your heart and how you feel towards your spouse if you let Him.

Today's Prayer

Dear Lord,

I acknowledge that I have not forgiven as You have commanded me to. Please forgive me Lord and wash me of my sin. Please help me to thoroughly entrust my spouse and the wrongs they have done against me into Your hands. I pray that Your will be done in our lives. Please help me to think on these wrongs no longer, but instead to focus my thoughts on You. Thank You for being the wonderful God that You are. Amen.

16

Master Your Rage

*"Get rid of all bitterness, rage, anger, harsh words, and
slander, as well as all types of evil behavior. Instead, be
kind to each other, tenderhearted, forgiving one another,
just as God through Christ has forgiven you."*
Ephesians 4:31-32 (NLT)

*"Stop being angry! Turn from your rage! Do not lose your
temper - it only leads to harm."*
Psalms 37:8 (NLT)

☙✄❧

It is very common to experience many levels of
anger and rage after finding out about your spouse's
affair. You must not let this anger take over your life, or
let it dwell in you until it becomes bitterness. If you leave
this rage unchecked, it will wreak havoc in your marriage
and drive a bigger wedge between you and your spouse.
Don't allow this anger and rage to take over your common
sense. What you do with your anger makes the
difference, never act on your emotions. When you feel
trapped, don't let your anger take over. Pray for the Lord
to rid you of the anger, rage and bitterness that consumes
you.

When you find yourself facing triggers (things that
remind you of the affair) that cause the pain, anger and
bitterness to resurface; you must learn to remind yourself
of your choice to forgive and commit to this choice with

every new trigger. This will be very hard at the beginning but keep doing it until it becomes a habit.

Be sure to be honest with your spouse when you are having triggers. Talking them out is the best way to defuse them. Just be sure that you are not being accusatory or judgmental when explaining what you are feeling. The more honest you both are with each other, the better you both will feel. You will be amazed at how much lighter you feel when you talk it out, instead of burying it deep inside you.

To conquer our rage we must learn to have compassion. Compassion is an important part of love. Compassion is the sharing of another's suffering and hurt. I know this is very difficult to hear, but your spouse is hurting too. It's not the same hurt, but it is hurt just the same. When we have compassion and understanding of their hurt, forgiveness and grace follow naturally behind. Trust me, this is not easy and can only be done through the grace of God.

Today's Prayer

Dear Lord,

Only You know how angry I am inside. You know how I struggle to trust You, to let You take charge of my life. Forgive me and help me turn my anger into compassion, my bitterness into forgiveness and my rage into love. Help me live the way You would have me live. Thank You for being the wonderful God that You are. Amen.

17

Expectations

"Do not judge others, and you will not be judged. For you will be treated as you treat others. The standard you use in judging is the standard by which you will be judged."
Matthew 7:1-2 (NLT)

What happens when you expect someone else to act and behave in a certain way? If they act the way you want them to then you are usually happy, but if they disappoint you then you are hurt, upset, or angry. We tend to gauge our emotions on what another has or hasn't done, but really our emotions or feelings come from our own expectations. A lot of the time our happiness hinges on our own expectations. If your spouse is doing everything you expect them to do then you're a happy camper, but watch out when they don't meet your expectations.

Having an expectation in itself is not wrong. But we must watch ourselves against being judgmental, or critical in a damaging way. How did Jesus respond to his disciples when they did not live up to their promises? He responded with compassion, understanding and with love. You won't find Him meeting unmet expectations with annoyance or anger like we tend to do.

It is very hard to respond to infidelity with compassion, understanding and love. In fact, the only way to accomplish this is through God. There is no way I could ever do that on my own. We have every right to expect our spouse to be faithful in our marriage. When they aren't, we have every right to be hurt and upset, but not a right to be judgmental against our spouse. This took me a very long time to wrap my mind around and to stop feeling so righteous when comparing myself to my husband.

Only God has the right to judge another. There was a part of me that felt I was better than my husband since I had never been unfaithful, but I soon realized I was being very judgmental. We should never have a holier than thou attitude toward anyone. What worked for me was to see my husband through God's eyes. I made myself do this often and even wrote down how I thought God saw my husband. God can help you to see your spouse through His eyes. All you need to do is ask and listen for His voice.

Today's Prayer

Dear Lord,

I thank You for Your perfect, loving nature. I desperately long to be more like You. I long to see my spouse with Your eyes of love and compassion. Help me to submit my thoughts to You. Please forgive my judgmental thoughts. I know that You are in control and that You will see me through this hard time. Thank You for being the wonderful God that You are. Amen.

18

What is Love?

"Love is patient and kind. Love is not jealous or boastful
or proud or rude. It does not demand its own way. It is not
irritable, and it keeps no record of being wronged. It does
not rejoice about injustice but rejoices whenever the truth
wins out. Love never gives up, never loses faith, is always
hopeful, and endures through every circumstance."
1 Corinthians 13:4-7 (NLT)

I always thought love was that heart swelling,
wonderful feeling I got inside towards my husband. To me
that was love. Even after 12 years of marriage I still had
those swelling emotions. But since he told me about his
affair I haven't felt that swelling of emotion. I assumed
since I no longer felt this "love" that I must no longer be
"in love" with him. I even told him that I no longer loved
him.

I think many of us have confused love with
infatuation. I believe this is why we hear "I love you but
I'm not in love with you" so often when it comes to affairs.
This is why those caught up in affairs believe they are "in
love" with the other person. But folks, that isn't love
that's just hormones kicking in. So, what is real love?

The <u>Message Bible</u> says this about love:

- Love never gives up.
- Love cares more for others than for self.

- Love doesn't want what it doesn't have.
- Love doesn't strut, or have a swelled head
- Love doesn't force itself on others,
- Love isn't always about "me first,"
- Love doesn't fly off the handle,
- Love doesn't keep score of the sins of others,
- Love doesn't revel when others grovel,
- Love takes pleasure in the flowering of truth,
- Love puts up with anything, and always trusts God
- Love always looks for the best, and never looks back but keeps going to the end.

Basically, love is what we do.   Today's society encourages us to get rid of those in our lives who make our lives difficult.   I'm sure you've had plenty of those telling you to divorce your wayward spouse.   True love tolerates when we feel it would be easier to just give up. Don't evaluate your relationship with your spouse according to your current emotional mood.   Your emotional status has nothing to do with what love is and how you should be relating to your spouse.

Today's Prayer

Dear Lord,
        Please fill me with Your unfailing love so that I may, through You, show love towards my spouse. Please reveal to me what true love really is. Help me to accurately reflect the love You show to us by my actions toward my spouse and help me to love with Your unconditional love. Thank You for being the wonderful God that You are. Amen.

19

Spiritual Rejuvenation

"Then he opened their minds to understand the Scriptures."
Luke 24:45 (NLT)

"The Lord is gracious and full of compassion, slow to anger and abounding in mercy and loving-kindness."
Psalm 145:8 (Amplified Bible)

Are you feeling like you might not have the energy to complete this healing journey you are on? I really thought it would never end, that I would not have the strength to make it to the end. Some days I had no energy at all, and I wanted to give up. I guess I felt that if I gave up, all the emotional turmoil would disappear. But that is far from the truth. Even if you leave your spouse, or even leave town, the pain stays inside you. We must work through the pain. There is no other way to heal.

You will find, though, that the road to recovery is much smoother if you really work on building your spiritual life. You will find that it will give you the power to overcome the emotional energy that is draining out of you. You will be pleased to notice that building up your spiritual life gives you an outside source to draw energy from. The more you praise and worship the Lord, the more energized you'll feel. I have found that when you really don't feel like praising the Lord, that is when you need to the most.

Here are some ways you can start working on building up your spiritual life. 1) Re-dedicate your life to the Lord. 2) Join a prayer or bible group. 3) Attend church regularly. 4) Find some mature Christians who can be mentors to you. 5) Find one or two same-sex Christian friends that are safe to confide in, and will help you by encouraging you and praying for you.

In order for you to build up your spiritual life you must make time to pray daily. This is how you talk to God. You can tell Him anything. Tell Him your fears, worries, needs and frustrations. Always be honest. Be sure to spend quality alone time with God and allow Him to speak to your heart. You can learn more about prayer, healing, and living a life that pleases Him by reading your bible. I would start with Proverbs, Psalms or John.

Today's Prayer

Dear Lord,

I'm so glad that You are in control of my life. I believe in You and I love You. I want to draw closer to You and I want a stronger spiritual life. Please help me to understand, and learn from, what I read in Your Word. Thank You for being the wonderful God that You are. Amen.

20

Does God Hear My Prayers?

"Be prepared. You're up against far more than you can handle on your own. Take all the help you can get, every weapon God has issued, so that when it's all over but the shouting you'll still be on your feet. Truth, righteousness, peace, faith, and salvation are more than words. Learn how to apply them. You'll need them throughout your life. God's Word is an indispensable weapon. In the same way, prayer is essential in this ongoing warfare. Pray hard and long."
Ephesians 6:13-18 (The Message)

Do you ever find yourself stumbling over your words and at a total loss of what to say when you're praying? Do you ever wonder if you're praying right? Do you ever pray but feel nothing? I have done all the above. I spent a long time praying and asking God to please make His presence be known to me, but still I felt nothing. Like no one was really listening. I think it was me who wasn't listening. So, how does one pray?

Praying isn't about saying the precise words or asking the right questions. Praying is about drawing yourself closer to God by just talking to Him like you would your best friend. You don't have to have fancy words or the "right" prayer for God to hear you. But, the most important thing is to learn to be quiet so that you can hear the small voice in your spirit that I call "Godly Whispers".

Get in a habit of meditating over His Word. Be very still, and quiet your mind so that you can hear those "Godly Whispers". The Holy Spirit will begin to lead your thoughts and your prayers. Pray that God will send His Holy Spirit to dwell in you, and that you might discern His voice from all the other voices.

Praying God's promises back to Him will give you a sense of confidence and direction when you don't know what to say when you're praying. Find your favorite verses where God promises you hope and pray those verses back to Him. You will find your prayers full of power, and you will have faith that God is able and willing to accomplish everything you are praying for.

Today's Prayer

Dear Lord,

Thank You so much that I don't have to have fancy words and special prayers to talk with You. Thank You for the gift of the Holy Spirit that lives inside me and guides me in my prayers and my walk with You. Thank You for the "Godly Whispers" that You send me when I am being still and quiet. Lord, please send me a verse that I can pray so that I can see Your Word come alive in my life and marriage. Thank You for being the wonderful God that You are. Amen.

21

Do You Like Being The Victim?

<u>Please read John 5:1-15</u>

"I can't, sir," the sick man said, "for I have no one to put me into the pool when the water bubbles up. Someone else always gets there ahead of me."
John 5:7 (NLT)

൭ᔛᚪᔚ൭

Are you destroyed by your fear, apprehension, dismay, hopelessness, isolation or self-pity? Do you believe that you're just a victim of your circumstances? Do you find that you enjoy playing the role of victim? Are you becoming accustomed to your sorrow? Do you love the process of healing so much that you don't really want to get healed? The man in the story above also had the victim mentality that so many of us fall prey too.

I grasped onto my victim role with all my might. Instead of getting better, I convince myself that I was worse. I found that playing the victim was working for me. People felt sorry for me and tried to comfort me. They were on my side since I had been the one that was wronged. When I played the victim role it made my husband hurt, and I enjoyed that. I wanted to make him hurt the way he hurt me. As we have learned, getting even doesn't work. It wasn't working. It wasn't making the pain and hurt go away, or bringing me happiness like I thought it would. I had become so good at convincing myself that I was a victim that the only logical reaction was anger.

If you don't fight to get back on your feet, or stop blaming others for your misery, you are allowing yourself to be sucked into a victim mentality that will turn into an addiction. You want to fight to break free of your prison of fear, pain, misery and total despair. The first step is surrendering your fear, self-pity, and grief to God.

You need to open your heart to God and His Word. The more you read God's Word, the more He will speak to your heart all of the promises of hope and healing He has for you. All you have to do to claim these promises of hope and healing is to surrender all your fear, self-pity, and grief into God's hands and trust that He will take care of you and will never leave you. We know He has a plan for our lives (**Jeremiah 29:11**) and a purpose for our pain. Remember, our purpose is not to understand (**Proverbs 3:5-6**) but to just have faith in our Father.

Today's Prayer

Dear Lord,

Lord, please take away my pain and remove anything in my life that hinders my relationship with You. Please show me the great plans You have for me. I give myself wholly to You, Lord. I no longer want to be a victim so please fill me with Your spirit and help me take that first step in surrendering all my fears to You. Thank You for being the wonderful God that You are. Amen.

22

Morning Blues?

*"God's loyal love couldn't have run out, his merciful love
couldn't have dried up. They're created new every
morning. How great your faithfulness! I'm sticking with
God (I say it over and over). He's all I've got left."*
Lamentations 3:22-24 (The Message)

After I found out about my husband's affair it
seemed that every morning was torture for me. Memories
would flood my mind, and black despair would fill my soul.
I found it very difficult just to get out of bed every morning.
But it doesn't have to be this way. God's mercy and grace
are fresh and new every morning; as sure as the sun rises
He is there offering us His grace. All we need to do is ask
and receive it.

God will never let you down. He is always there
right beside you with every up and down, twist and turn of
this roller coaster ride you have found yourself on. When
you are confused, hurt and in total despair He is there to
help you. He will always stay faithful to you. Morning after
morning His awesome grace is there for you. Let Him fill
your soul with peace and comfort. The hard part is
learning how to receive what God is offering us.
Sometimes we don't feel worthy. We must learn to
receive and be very thankful for what God has promised
us.

It seems to me that God is saying no matter how awful our life is today, there is a brand new day coming tomorrow. You will have more good days than bad ones as time goes on. Soon, you will put enough of those good days together to get you past the despair you are feeling now. I know this is hard to imagine when you are feeling so devastated but know that it is true and it will happen.

This is probably the darkest time of your life, but please, never lose your hope. Know that tomorrow is a new day. Believe in the faithfulness of God. His compassion for you is a sure thing and it's never ending. Know that this awful thing that has happened to you and your marriage will not consume you as long as you look to God and His grace every day. Please set your eyes on His faithfulness right now. Only He can deliver you from this pain and anguish.

Today's Prayer

Dear Lord,

Thank You so much for Your renewed grace every morning! I am so thankful that Your love never runs out. Lord, I'm surrendering my sadness to You and asking for You to fill my spirit with peace and compassion. I am putting my whole trust in Your faithfulness, because I know You will be beside me through this whole ordeal. Thank You for being the wonderful God that You are. Amen.

23

There is Hope

"May the God of hope fill you with all joy and peace as you trust in him, so that you may overflow with hope by the power of the Holy Spirit."
Romans 15:13 (NIV)

"You will be rewarded for this; your hope will not be disappointed."
Proverbs 23:18 (NLT)

Do you feel there is no hope left in your marriage? I'm sure there are days when you feel utterly hopeless and alone, but I am here to tell you there is hope. The source of all our hope is through God. From God alone flows all our hope, peace and joy. You can find a whole new and happier marriage in Gods loving plan.

Many people that I have spoken with are struggling with the issue of hope, especially those that have recently just found out. Many feel there is no hope left for their marriage since their spouse's have been unfaithful. They can't see how their marriage can be repaired after something so devastating. Even I felt this way after I found out. I truly thought there was no other way than divorce. I just couldn't fathom staying with someone that could do that to me. It's a horrible feeling; to feel like all hope is lost.

Did you know there are people out there with no hope that are willing to pay any amount of money to anyone offering them even a glimmer of hope? If only they knew that God has all the hope they will ever need and it's free, all they need to do is ask. God is the "God of Hope" and He wants to fill you with His joy, peace and love. All you have to do is put your faith and trust in Him and you will find yourself to be brimming over with hope. Hope means, "I know I can make it." It's actually amazing how far we can go on just a little bit of hope.

We may be powerless to create change in our situation, but with God nothing is impossible. When our faith is waning, God strengthens and renews us. When we trust Him we remain in His peace but when we don't trust Him we find anxiety and fear in our hearts. Please, won't you put your trust in God today to heal your marriage and send you renewed hope?

Today's Prayer

Dear Lord,

Thank You so much for Your Word that speaks to me words of hope. Forgive me for ever doubting that there is no hope for my marriage. Right now, I claim Your Word for my marriage and my life. Thank You for the promise of a good future that I know You will give me because You fulfill Your promises. Thank You for being the wonderful God of hope that You are. Amen.

24

How Do I Release My Hurt?

"Forget about what's happened; don't keep going over old history. Be alert, be present. I'm about to do something brand-new. It's bursting out! Don't you see it?"
Isaiah 43:18-19 (The Message)

I struggled for over 2 years searching for the answer to this question. I asked our marriage coach, I searched the self-help books, I perused the online forums but I just couldn't find the answer to this one question. I didn't want the answer of "time heals all wounds". That was the main one I heard over and over. That wasn't doing me any good at that moment in time. I wish I knew then what I know now, because I would have known to turn to the Bible for all my answers instead of the world. When I finally turned to the Word, I realized that only surrendering to God, my devastating pain and hurt, could I be released from it.

God tells us in His Word that we are to stop focusing on what is lost and what has happened in the past. We are to start focusing on all the new things God will be and is doing in our lives and marriages. We are to stop obsessing over the affair and all the gory details and force ourselves to focus on what is presently going on in our marriage today. This might be the hardest thing for you to do right now. You may have to force yourself to refocus on God's plan for your life and marriage several times a day. When you find yourself caught in that obsessive cycle, cry out to God. He will deliver you from the negative thoughts and bring new peaceful thoughts to you. The more you read the Word of God the easier this will be. He will bring back to mind all His promises, but first, you must have read them.

The pain of infidelity never just goes away, time will not bring full and complete healing. You will find that every time you think about the affair, you will *feel* the pain. We can't let go of the past without receiving the new from God. You can't do one without the other. But God must have full control of your entire heart before He can heal it. (**Jeremiah 29:13**) So, if you're still hurting then cry out to the Lord and ask Him to heal your wounded bleeding heart. Allow your eyes and your ears to be open to the message God wants you to receive.

Today's Prayer

Dear Lord,

Please send Your healing today. Allow the Holy Spirit to touch and heal my body, soul and spirit. Please help me with my obsessive thoughts of my spouse's affair and fill me instead with peaceful and loving thoughts. Thank You for Your wonderful peace and Your never ending love for me. Thank You for all the new and wonderful things You have planned for my life and my marriage. Thank You for being the wonderful God that You are. Amen.

25

Realize That God Is Always With You

"The Lᴏʀᴅ hears his people when they call to him for help. He rescues them from all their troubles. The Lᴏʀᴅ is close to the brokenhearted; he rescues those whose spirits are crushed."
Psalms 34:17-18 (NLT)

Did you know that the Lord hears your cries for help and He knows the agony you face every day while you try to heal from the aftermath of your spouse's affair? The Lord promises to release you from all your troubles. Do you really believe this with all your heart? Are you putting your trust in God alone to heal your marriage and family?

Did you ever notice that when you're facing a hardship in your life that you tend to feel very alone in it? There are many out there who, after finding out about their spouse's affair, feel like they are the only ones going through this. They feel like they are all alone in their pain. If ever I were crushed in spirit, it would have to be this period in my life. Even though we may feel alone in our pain, this is when the Lord draws us close to Him.

When our hearts are in shards around our feet, He is right there to bring us comfort and healing. Because of your intense pain you may not always feel His presence. That doesn't mean He has forgotten you or left you to fend for yourself. He is always right there with you, whether you feel His presence or not. He never leaves you alone, especially in your time of desperate need. He is ready and willing to pour His love into your shattered heart and breathe life back into your broken spirit.

I believe that God uses our pain so that we may draw closer to Him. Sometimes pain is vital to get our attention. Many people don't believe in the biblical truths until they experience pain. If our lives were perfect would we feel that we needed God? If we never hurt would we ever cry out to Him? If we never stumble would we ever ask Him to help us up?

Always remember that as you are going through this devastating ordeal in your life, the Lord hears and sees your pain and He wants to heal you from all this devastation. I want you to cry out to Him right now and know with your whole being that the Lord will heal your wounded heart and crushed spirit.

Today's Prayer

Dear Lord,
I cry out to You, Lord, please heal me from all my pain and anguish. I place my sorrow in Your hands. Lord, please wrap your arms around me and surround me with Your love and compassion. Thank You for being close to me while I am broken hearted and for saving me while I am crushed in spirit. Thank You for being the friend I so desperately need in the midst of my brokenness and despair. Thank You for being the wonderful God that You are. Amen.

26

The Pain Lasts Longer Than Expected

"Be merciful to me, LORD, for I am faint; O LORD, heal me, for my bones are in agony. My soul is in anguish. How long, O LORD, how long? Turn, O LORD, and deliver me; save me because of your unfailing love."
Psalms 6:2-4 (NIV)

"I am worn out from sobbing. All night I flood my bed with weeping, drenching it with my tears. My vision is blurred by grief."
Psalm 6:6-7 (NLT)

Struggling to heal from a spouse's affair can have you making unexpected turns that will throw you up and down over and over again. It may even feel that for every step forward, you take at least three back. The healing process takes longer than you, or I, ever imagined. Experts claim that it takes two to five years to fully heal from an affair. It's different for everyone. We each heal in our own time. It was 4½ years before I could say, "Yes, I have recovered."

You can't rush the healing process. I thought that by the two-year mark that I would be healed and we would be doing great, but that wasn't how it turned out. I became depressed because I thought I should have been much further along in my healing by then. I guess God wasn't done with me yet. Every single one of us has our own healing timeline.   Don't gauge your healing to someone else's.   Just know, whatever healing phase you are in is the right one for you, and what you are feeling is normal.   Everyone that has been through this has had the exact same feelings that you are having.   Think of your healing process not so much as getting rid of all your pain and hurt, but to have your marriage no longer controlled by them.

I want you to know that knowing the Lord and His comfort doesn't make the pain and hurt magically go away.   He is there to support you in the midst of your pain.   Here in **Psalm 6:2-4** we see that David is getting tired of the healing process and is crying out to the Lord.   But, you can see that he is leaving the timeline in God's hands.   This is my prayer for you, that you would put your entire healing process in God's hands and trust Him with it.

Today's Prayer

Dear Lord,

I am so filled with sorrow that I can't even imagine a healing timeline.   Thank You so much that I do not have to worry about it because it's all in Your hands.   Please send me comfort as I learn to lean on You and trust You with my healing process.   Thank You for teaching me how to draw closer to You in my time of need.   Thank You for being the wonderful God that You are.   Amen.

27

Lost Cause?

"Jesus was blunt: "No chance at all if you think you can pull it off by yourself. Every chance in the world if you let God do it."
Mark 10:27 (The Message)

"It was so bad we didn't think we were going to make it. We felt like we'd been sent to death row, that it was all over for us. As it turned out, it was the best thing that could have happened."
2 Corinthians 1:8-10 (The Message)

Are you feeling like your marriage is a lost cause and that you should just give up? Are you afraid that your marriage will never get over this giant hurdle and become a happy marriage again? In the early days after finding out about the affair, I felt all these things and more. I'm sure many others feel them also. For me, there has been a lot of healing between then and now. I can honestly say that YES your marriage can be happy again and so can you. You have to learn to lean on God and let Him heal your heart and your marriage.

I do pray that none of you give up on your marriage. Even if your spouse has, that doesn't mean you have to. Even if they left you for the other person this still doesn't mean that there isn't any hope for your marriage. You may feel that saving your marriage is impossible, but with God all things are possible, especially to those who believe. Please, don't listen to others, who think they are doing you a favor, when they tell you that your marriage is over, and to leave your spouse and file for divorce. Many people, including friends and family, told me this was the only choice I had. Today, I am so thankful that I didn't listen to any of them.

Do you need a miracle in your marriage? Pray for faith for nothing is too hard, or too big, for God. I challenge you to put aside your sorrow and sadness and choose to praise God in these, the darkest hours of your life. Remember that, in your own strength, overcoming infidelity would be near impossible but if you proclaim and believe that God can do anything, He can and He will. Put God's courage into your heart with the truth and promises of His Word.

Today's Prayer

Dear Lord,

I know that I cannot heal this marriage by myself. I am very thankful that my marriage has every chance in the world because I am placing my marriage into Your hands. Lord, please help me to walk in Your truth and Your light. Lead me in the way I should go. Please bless my marriage and make it whole again. Thank You for being the wonderful God that You are. Amen.

28

Showing Compassion

*"Let all bitterness and indignation and wrath (passion, rage,
bad temper) and resentment (anger, animosity) and quarreling
(brawling, clamor, contention) and slander (evil-speaking,
abusive or blasphemous language) be banished from you, with
all malice (spite, ill will, or baseness of any kind). And become
useful and helpful and kind to one another, tenderhearted
(compassionate, understanding, loving-hearted), forgiving one
another [readily and freely], as God in Christ forgave you."*
Ephesians 4:31-32 (Amplified Bible)

There were times in the first couple of years that I
let my husband have it. I was mean, nasty and hurtful on
purpose just to cause him pain. I now wish I could take all
of it back but I can't. Once, in a public restaurant I had a
fit and it was awful. You must learn, when information is
being revealed to you, not to respond with hateful words.
If you can't control yourself, go off by yourself and pray
until you are calm again. One of the hardest things for me
was to show compassion and understanding to my
husband after he betrayed me in such an awful way. God
says we are to become useful and helpful. Screaming,
yelling and being irate isn't being useful or helpful in the
recovery of our marriages.

How do we learn to accept what is being said, in
the form of details of the affair, and not explode? Before
you and your spouse talk about the affair, pray for the
strength to hear whatever their going say about it. Pray
that uncontrollable anger doesn't swell up inside you, and

that will be filled with an inner peace. It might sound impossible, but nothing is impossible with God. Be sure to ask only those questions to which you can hear the worst case scenario and not explode in anger.

There will be no emotional intimacy if you both are harboring resentments, bitterness, and anger. These emotions are very deadly to a relationship. The devil tries to use these emotions to push disorder into your marriage. You must resist the desire to use bitter, resentful, and abusive words because all you'll accomplish is to tear down your marriage. Your goal is to build it back up. I've heard it said that to disclaim your honest emotions isn't healthy, but neither is making a habit of "throwing up" the negative ones in the rouse of "honesty." Remember that letting go of resentments, bitterness and anger is something that we do for ourselves as much as it is for our spouse and our marriage.

Today's Prayer

Dear Lord,

Please help me control my anger and my tongue towards my spouse. Help me to accept the affair details calmly and not to explode in anger. I want to release my resentment, bitterness and anger to You, Lord, for only You can take these things from me and replace them with a calming peace and compassion that I so long to have. Thank You for never leaving me and for showering me with Your love and compassion. Thank You for being the wonderful God that You are. Amen.

29

Being Unable to Function

*"God's way is perfect. All the LORD's promises prove true.
He is a shield for all who look to him for protection."*
Psalms 18:30 (NLT)

Have you noticed since you found out about your spouse's affair, that your mind isn't letting you think about anything else? Do you find yourself totally consumed by the sheer grief of it all? Do you find that you aren't able to get much done during the day, and that every aspect of your life has been disrupted in more ways than you ever imagined? When I first found out, I couldn't do more than lay across my bed for hours at a time. I couldn't focus on anything and I found that I had lost my short-term memory. I just couldn't seem to function any more.

Isn't it nice to know that even though our world has been turned upside down and has lost all sense of order that Jesus never changes! Like it says in **Hebrews 13:8** *"Jesus Christ is the same yesterday, today, and forever."* Even though the world as you knew it exploded, and what you thought was black is now white, and what you thought was white is now black, God is the same and His way is perfect. All the promises He has given you in His Word will prove to be true. You can cling to His promises because they are there for you to bring you comfort and peace in the midst of all the chaos.

When you find yourself obsessing about the affair, and you can't seem to function normally throughout the day any more, look to God and use Him as a shield against all the bad thoughts you have racing through your mind. He can shield you from all those obsessive thoughts and help you get some normalcy back into your life. Every time you find yourself obsessing make yourself repeat one of God's promises and claim it with all your heart.

If you leave all your burdens and obsessive thoughts with Him, you will have your mind back to think about other more important and pleasant things. This won't happen overnight, but if you stay disciplined with your thoughts and keep praying, you can master them and they will no longer rule over you. The Key to this is diligence and prayer. The more you pray over your obsessive thoughts the quicker they will go away. God holds the key to your freedom; let Him unlock your prison door.

Today's Prayer

Dear Lord,

I am totally consumed by the grief and I am unable to control my obsessive thoughts on my own. Please take them from me and replace them with thoughts that are more peaceful and loving. I am asking for Your shield of protection over my thoughts so that negative ones can no longer rule my life. Thank You for Your wonderful promises that You have in store for me. Thank You for being the wonderful God that You are. Amen

30

Where Does Your Help Come From?

"I look up to the mountains; does my strength come from mountains? No, my strength comes from God, who made heaven, and earth, and mountains. He won't let you stumble; your Guardian God won't fall asleep. Not on your life! Israel's Guardian will never doze or sleep."
Psalms 121:1-4 (The Message)

The most difficult time to learn about affairs, and how they affect people, is when you are going through it yourself. This is your crash course, and the learning curve is fierce. It always seems that the right thing to do is the most difficult. If you seek to understand you will be better able to recover. The more you know about affairs the better understanding you will have about affairs and how they affect everyone. I got a lot of information from support groups, books, and online resources. I found solace in talking with others that were, or had been, in the same situation I was in.

Are you lost in your sorrow and feel like God is a million miles away? Cling to everything you know to be true about Him. Open your heart and mind for a deeper understanding of Him and His promises. Your strength isn't going to come from man, mountains, or anything worldly. Your strength is going to come from God who made everything. He's not here to watch you fall on your face, but to help you up and to watch over you and help you with your struggles.

Learn to take comfort in these verses. When you are fearful over your ordeal know that God is always watching over you and guarding you with His protection. He is available to you at any time of the day or night. No waiting in line, or on hold. He is there for you whenever you call out His name. Even if it feels like God is not listening He really is. Don't be fooled into thinking that God doesn't hear you because this is a lie.

Knowing this always made me sleep better. I knew I didn't have to worry and fret over my present circumstances. The more time you spend in His Word, in prayer and meditation the better you will start to feel. You will be amazed at the changes that will happen in your life and your marriage when you make a habit of doing these things. Be ready to be amazed!

Today's Prayer

Dear Lord,

Thank You for Your faithful loving care and guidance. Help me to remember this when I feel upset over the progress of my healing. Help me to remember that You are in control and not me, and that I don't need to worry about how things are going to work out. I just need to trust that they will. Thank You for watching over me and letting me rest in Your protective care. Thank You for being the wonderful God that You are. Amen.

31

Losing Identity

"This is how we know we're living steadily and deeply in him, and he in us: He's given us life from his life, from his very own Spirit. Also, we've seen for ourselves and continue to state openly that the Father sent his Son as Savior of the world. Everyone who confesses that Jesus is God's Son participates continuously in an intimate relationship with God. We know it so well, we've embraced it heart and soul, this love that comes from God."
1 John 4:13-16 (The Message)

When I found out about the affair I felt like everything I knew about my husband and marriage was a lie. Thoughts like, "What is real?" "Who am I?" or "Who is this man I married?" repeatedly swirled in my mind. I felt like the past whole year of our marriage was a complete lie. Do you find yourself asking these questions? Are you wondering who you are and who your spouse is? Do you wonder where you and your spouse went? Do you ever wonder if you will ever be the "old" you again. Do you wonder if you will ever see the person you married again?

It took me a while to accept the reality that my husband, my marriage, my family and myself were no longer the same. How do you find yourself again and does your spouse ever go back to what you thought them to be? How are you supposed to go on from here? I had every single one of these questions and probably much more. I'm sure you do as well.

There is hope and with the Lords help and your trust in Him you can find yourself again. This won't happen instantaneously, and it will probably be a very painful process. Always remember, through God everything is possible. God will be there every step of the way and He will guide you through the whole process. He will never leave you to suffer alone. As you learn to depend more on God, your relationship with Him will grow stronger.

The way back to self is through God, His Word and prayer. You may mourn for the person you once were, the one with innocent trust, but you'll emerge a stronger person with a closer relationship with God. It's okay to mourn the person you once were, the spouse you once had, and even what the marriage was before the affair, but understand that everything can come out better than it was. With God at the wheel miracles happen. Cling to Him, trust Him, believe in His promises and you'll find yourself, your spouse and your marriage again.

Today's Prayer

Dear Lord,

I'm so broken hearted, and there are days I don't know who I am anymore. Please piece my broken heart back together with Your never ending love. Lord, help me find myself again and let me see my spouse the way You do. Thank You for carrying me through these hard times and never leaving my side. Thank You for being the wonderful God that You are. Amen.

32

The Joy Does Return

*"I tell you the truth, you will weep and mourn while the
world rejoices. You will grieve, but your grief will turn to
joy."*
John 16:20 (NIV)

*"So you have sorrow now, but I will see you again; then
you will rejoice, and no one can rob you of that joy."*
John 16:22 (NLT)

Believe it or not, you will get better. You will
experience joy in your life again. I know it's hard to
believe right now, but take it from someone that has been
there—it does get better. You will not be forever lost in
this painful darkness. You will find your joy again and
there will be days where you will laugh and smile again.
Don't be fooled into thinking that happiness will never be
yours again. It will take time and sometimes the process
is so slow it feels like we'll never be happy again. But
trust in the fact that each day you are moving towards
healing because you are moving towards God.

I thought I would never smile, laugh or feel
happiness again, but after a while, with a lot of inner work
and prayer, things really did start getting better. You
might think I'm crazy, but you will actually have days that
the affair won't enter your mind and you will find yourself
happy, thinking good thoughts about the future. This

doesn't happen overnight, and it didn't even happen to me in the first 2½ years, but it does happen. Please don't be disheartened, remember that it takes a *minimum* of 2 years to heal. By 5 years you will experience joy again, and the affair will no longer be the only thing you can think about.

When you start to notice that you're having more good days than bad days, rejoice and thank the Lord because you know that you are really are healing. Rejoice in every good day, or even every good hour, that you have. Thank the Lord for all the good feelings you have as they all come from Him. God is the source of all our hope and joy. Praise Him every time you feel even the slightest bit of joy. It may seem that everyone around you is happy while you are down, but this is a trick your mind plays on you. This is your time to mourn, but your grief will turn to joy again, as long as you cling to His Word and claim His promises as your own.

Today's Prayer

Dear Lord,

I can't even remember what peace, joy and happiness feels like, but I believe that You will turn my sorrow into peace, joy and happiness that no one can take away from me. I am putting my full trust in You. I do not expect to heal overnight but I know that You are healing me every day. Thank You for promising the return of my peace and joy, and I will cling to Your promises as my own. Thank You for being the wonderful God that You are. Amen.

33

Finding Comfort

"God blesses those who mourn, for they will be comforted."
Matthew 5:4 (NLT)

"When I walk into the thick of trouble, keep me alive in the angry turmoil. With one hand strike my foes, with your other hand save me. Finish what you started in me, GOD. Your love is eternal—don't quit on me now."
Psalm 138:7 (The Message)

This is an exciting promise given to us by the Lord. He has given us all hope. In those first weeks I felt like I had lost so much. I actually mourned for the marriage I had lost, for I knew it would never again be the same again. I had lost faith in my husband. I also lost respect for my husband. Many betrayed spouses feel these feelings. A part of you dies, and you are feeling that it will never come back. Don't fall for these lies. You can regain the trust and respect back, it is not gone forever. A lot will depend on the actions of your spouse but God plays an even bigger role in the trust and respect department.

Your emotions can really hit you hard, and they can come at the most unexpected times. You might be doing all right; not even thinking about the affair, and then suddenly, some little tiny thing happens and brings it all flooding back. It actually feels like the first day all over again. When things like this happen, let the Lord console your mind and calm the storm that is raging within you. One of the great things about Jesus is that He can relate with grief. *"He was despised and rejected—a man of sorrows, acquainted with deepest grief."* Isaiah 53:3 (NLT)

The Lord knows the pain you are feeling. He wants to hold you tight to Him while you are weathering this storm. He is here to bring you peace and calm. No one should live his or her life in pain and sorrow. Jesus has come to turn your mourning into joy during this time that you are broken hearted and feeling betrayed. Jesus is your comforter. His promise that you would be comforted has lasting returns. Remember, God doesn't want you to be in pain forever. He wants you to experience His comfort and love and it's all there just for the asking.

Today's Prayer

Dear Lord,

Please send Your love and comfort to me. I know You will heal me, and make it so that I am able to live in joy again. Thank You for Your promise of blessings and comfort, I will claim them as my own. Lord, draw me closer to You and help me to truly understand my need for You. Thank You for being the wonderful God that You are. Amen.

34

Starting The Healing Journey

"What a God we have! And how fortunate we are to have him, this Father of our Master Jesus! Because Jesus was raised from the dead, we've been given a brand-new life and have everything to live for, including a future in heaven—and the future starts now! God is keeping careful watch over us and the future. The Day is coming when you'll have it all—life healed and whole."
1 Peter 1:3-5 (The Message)

After a month I had had enough. I wanted the pain to go away and I wanted the constant 24/7 obsessive thoughts of them together to stop. I just wanted it all to stop and be "normal" again. If there had been a magic pill to take to make this happen I would have taken it. But I now know there is no "easy button" to getting over a betrayal like this. You have to go through the whole process no matter how hard it is or how much you don't want to. The only way to fully recover is to travel through the pain. Not over it, under it, or around it, but through it. There are no short cuts in recovery. You can never ignore the pain and pretend it's not there because it will never go away until you deal with it head on.

I want you, at this very moment, to make a commitment to yourself to begin the healing process. If you want to be fully recovered then this must be done. Dealing with your spouse's affair is a lot like going through someone's death. You must force yourself to move forward, even if your whole being is telling you otherwise. You may even feel as if you can't handle this journey and you want to just run away from it all but be encouraged! God will take you right where you're at now. You are never beyond hope with Him. God accepts you for who you are right now and He will gently mold you with His loving hands. Remember, no one is a ever a lost cause with God.

You must prepare your mind for action. No more letting your mind obsess about the affair. Take control of your negative thoughts, don't let them control you. Force yourself to be positive in whatever ways you can. Remember you are not in a hopeless situation. Set your hope fully in God, knowing He can do all things-even the impossible. God is always there waiting for you to come to Him so that He can bring you comfort and peace. God is waiting with arms open wide to envelope you with His love. Run to Him with your feelings of pain and hopelessness. Leave them at His feet and feel His comfort fill your soul.

Today's Prayer

Dear Lord,
I know that it is only by Your grace that I can be healed. I am going to commit my healing journey to You and I promise that I will not give up. Thank You for being with me every step of the way. Lord, please help me have a positive attitude every day, and help me control my obsessive thoughts. I will place my hope fully in You. Thank You for being the wonderful God that You are. Amen.

35

Don't Push It Down

"The Lord is my Strength and my [impenetrable] Shield; my heart trusts in, relies on, and confidently leans on Him, and I am helped; therefore my heart greatly rejoices, and with my song will I praise Him. The Lord is my [unyielding] Strength, and He is the Stronghold of salvation to [me] His anointed."
Psalm 28:7-8 (Amplified Bible)

Are you finding yourself pushing down emotions you don't feel like dealing with? Do you feel that they are just too painful to deal with right now? Do you think if you push them down long enough, that they'll just go away? I'm the queen of pushing emotions down. I can push down a negative emotion until I think it's all gone. Don't be fooled as I was because they are still there. Emotions you push down never really go away. These pushed down emotions can and will eat you alive. You can actually become physically sick by doing this.

It's necessary to go through the grieving process to heal. You can't push down your sorrow, pain and heartache and expect to truly heal. You will not ever truly heal if you push your pain away. Please don't run from the pain. Even though it is excruciatingly painful right now, you need to face the pain head on so that you can move forward with your recovery. Stuffing down your pain is a way of denying that it exists. This may be one of the hardest things you'll ever do, but know that you do not have to travel this road alone. God is there for you and He wants to hold your hand every step of the way. Whenever you need Him, He is right there. He never leaves you alone.

When you are in pain, learn to cry out to God and tell Him everything you're feeling. Making this a habit instead of other means of coping like; shopping, eating or drinking. Reaching out to God instead will make your healing journey a lot shorter. Be sure to tell God all about your anguish. Tell Him your concerns and fears, holding nothing back. God is there for you any time you need Him. He wants to wrap His arms around you and make you feel safe and loved. God is there to bring you out of your distress. This is God's promise to you, so embrace it knowing He is there for you to lean on. You are never alone, even when you feel utterly alone, you are not.

Today's Prayer

Dear Lord,

I am crying out to You, Lord, because I don't know what to do with all this pain and heartache. I am willing to give them to You. Help me to never push my emotions down but to bring them to You so that I can be healed from them. Thank You for the promise of delivering me from my distress and pain. I will learn to lean on You instead of pushing my emotions down. Thank You for being the wonderful God that You are. Amen.

36

Finding Your Way

"Your Word is a lamp to my feet and a light for my path."
Psalms 119:105 (NIV)

"I [the Lord] will instruct you and teach you in the way you should go; I will counsel you with My eye upon you."
Psalm 32:8 (Amplified Bible)

Healing from a spouse's affair is a long hard process that literally takes years. Don't let anyone ever tell you different. There is no quick fix about healing from affairs. Those that seem to heal over night didn't really process the whole thing and aren't really healed. They may look happy and healed, but they are just good at shoving down their emotions. Don't look at healing as a goal you can only reach once you finish this journey because each tiny success is part of your healing. Celebrate all your successes, no matter how small they may seem, be sure to acknowledge that they are successes.

Do you ever wonder how in the world you're going to get from where you are right now to becoming fully recovered? Does it seem impossible? I am here to tell you that you don't have to worry about how you're going to get there. You don't have to see the end of the road; you only need to see a few feet in front of you to keep moving forward. Just as if you had to walk a mile in pitch-black darkness. You can make it safely by just by seeing only a few feet in front of you with a flash light. It's the same with God's Word because His Word is a lamp unto your feet and it's a light for your path. It's all you need to get from point A to point B safely.

Where are you in your healing journey? Are you clinging to God along the way? Do you turn to Him when you stumble and fall? Do you cry out to Him when you no longer can take the pain and heartache? Did you know that God has already placed your healing in His hands? Where ever you are in your healing journey God is there and ready to take the journey with you. Isn't it wonderful that you don't have to take this long and very difficult journey alone? God will direct your path and tell you which way to turn. He alone is your navigator.

Today's Prayer

Dear Lord,

Please be the light I need to make it to the end of this long hard journey I am on. I know that it's only because of You that I can even make this journey. I know I may stumble and fall, but I also know that You will be there to help me back up. I am turning over my healing to You Lord, to place in Your hands. I no longer need to worry about it. Thank You for directing my path and showing me the best way to go. Thank You for being the wonderful God that You are. Amen.

37

Are You In A Hurry?

"How long must I struggle with anguish in my soul, with sorrow in my heart every day? How long will my enemy have the upper hand?"
Psalms 13:2 (NLT)

I remember comparing myself to others. I would think how unfair it was that they were so much further along in their recovery than I was. I would beat myself up for not being further along than I thought I should be. I was in an all fire hurry to be able to say that I was "fully recovered." When I want something I want it right now. I'm not very patient but I am working on that every day. Comparing myself to others was causing me to be very depressed and slowed my recovery down.

I thought that at 1 year out I would no longer hurt or obsess, but I found out that was wrong. At 2 years out, I thought I would be totally healed and my marriage would be normal again. Wrong! I was very upset at the 2-year mark when I was still having painful triggers and my marriage wasn't doing very well. It was then that I decided to give myself the time I needed to heal. I would no longer be upset that I wasn't doing as well as I thought I should be. I said to myself that I would give myself the whole 5 years, and then look at how I felt because it takes from 2-5 years to fully recover from an affair.

You will find that your path to recovery cannot be compared to someone else's path. You are going to heal in your own way and in your own time. The path to recovery doesn't have a set timeline. If you rush the healing process you will get the opposite effect. I can tell you that healing from affairs is a process, not a "do this once and you're done" kind of deal. It is a much longer process than any of us really want to believe. Your healing journey is your own and no one else's.

Thankfully, you are not alone in it. Do not be afraid to cry out to God and ask Him, "How long must I struggle with anguish in my soul, with sorrow in my heart every day?" God knows your struggles and He knows your pain like no one else on earth. Keep reading your Bible, praying and leaning on Him. Don't worry about where you "think" you should be in your recovery right now. God works in His time not yours. As long as you are obeying God then you are right where you are supposed to be.

Today's Prayer

Dear Lord,

I am feeling so very isolated, vulnerable, abandoned and alone. Teach me to depend upon You. Please give me the faith to overcome my fears and the strength to defeat my sorrow. Help me to accept that my road to recovery will be a long hard one, but one I can do with You by my side. Help me to not rush my healing but to take things slow and accept all the baby steps in my recovery. Thank You for being the wonderful God that You are. Amen.

38

Are Other's Helping or Hurting?

*"Then Job spoke again: "I have heard all this before.
What miserable comforters you are! Won't you ever stop
blowing hot air? What makes you keep on talking? I
could say the same things if you were in my place. I could
spout off criticism and shake my head at you. But if it
were me, I would encourage you. I would try to take away
your grief."*
Job 16:1-5 (NLT)

There will be times when other people, including your own spouse, will try to give you advice or constructive criticism. I know many betrayed spouses that are very hurt with comments like, "Why can't you just get over it?" I have also had people tell me "It's been (put in a time) already, shouldn't you be over it by now?" Comments like these can cause us great pain. Sometimes you can't count on people to say just the right thing to make you feel better. You can always count on God's wisdom and love to make you feel better.

You can hear Job's frustration here with people telling him what he should do and how he should feel. These people didn't understand what Job was really going through. It's the same way with the people that make comments to you. No one really understands your pain even those that have been through it themselves. This is because everyone's marriage is unique but those who have been through a spouse's affair are the best ones to seek help from. Even your spouse has no real clue of the intense pain that you are in. They can try to empathize but they will really never know your pain. This is why it's so important to find others that have been through what you have been through. People who will truly empathize and understand your pain and will NEVER tell you to just "get over it already". They will help you any way they can because they know this kind of pain.

Remember, you have an understanding of the healing process that other people just don't have. You know that the recovery process is different for everyone. You know that you have to let the healing process take its own pace, because if you try to speed it up you will only be hindering your healing. When you hear these comments, take your pain to the Lord and tell Him how much this hurts you. Don't keep the pain to yourself, but cry out to the Lord for He knows the pain that you are in. God is the Master Healer and He wants to deliver you from this awful pain.

Today's Prayer

Dear Lord,

I know these people mean well, but they are hurting me terribly with their comments. Help me to release the pain they are causing me and to have a forgiving spirit towards them. Thank You Lord for being my comforter and my refuge during the harsh storms that life is throwing my way. Thank You for being the wonderful God that You are. Amen.

39

Roller Coaster Ride

"God's way is perfect. All the LORD's promises prove true. He's a shield for all who look to him for protection. For who is God except the LORD? Who but our God is a solid rock? God is my strong fortress, and He makes my way perfect."
2 Samuel 22:31-33 (NLT)

"Don't waver in resolve. Don't fear. Don't hesitate. Don't panic. GOD, your God, is right there with you, fighting with you against your enemies, fighting to win."
Deuteronomy 20:3-4 (The Message)

Have you ever heard that recovery is like being on a roller coaster ride? Has it felt that way for you? Do you notice your emotions change unpredictably? You have times when you are doing all right, and then all of a sudden something triggers you and you find yourself spiraling down again. You become filled with fear, depression, anger, loneliness, and despair. You may notice that these emotions come and go and make your life feel like a roller coaster ride that you can't get off of.

I know you want to get off this horrible ride as do many others. There were many times I just wanted to throw my hands up and scream, "I quit!" Oh, how I wanted to give up. I had thoughts of running away and never looking back. I thought things would never get any better, but thankfully I was wrong. Trust me, stay the course. Remember, you can't hurry the healing process. Every time a trigger happens and you pray through it, process it and even talk about it with your spouse, is a sign that you are recovering. You will begin to see that you are on the upward track much more than the downward spiral.

Being on this roller coaster ride can make you feel out of control and no one likes to feel this way. Take comfort in knowing that God is always in control, even when you're not. He is your solid rock, unmoving and unchanging. He will keep you steady when you feel your life is crazy and unmanageable. God is your constant when life right now is anything but constant. He will support you the whole time you are on this crazy ride. He will protect you and keep you from falling off. All you have to do is put your trust in God knowing He will keep you safe and will bring you back to safety.

Today's Prayer

Dear Lord,

I want to make it to the end of this ride, and I know with You I will be able to make it through all the ups and downs. Thank You for being my solid rock for which I can find solid ground. Thank You for being my strong fortress, and making my way perfect. Thank You for being the wonderful God that You are. Amen.

40

The Black Hole

"Even to your old age and gray hairs I am he, I am he who will sustain you. I have made you and I will carry you; I will sustain you and I will rescue you."
Isaiah 46:4 (NIV)

"The Lord is good, a Strength and Stronghold in the day of trouble; He knows (recognizes, has knowledge of, and understands) those who take refuge and trust in Him."
Nahum 1:7 (Amplified Bible)

Have you ever noticed that when the numbness has worn off, and some of the anger has subsided, all you're left with is a deep gut-wrenching pain? Have you ever felt like you're spiraling down this deep black hole and no matter how hard you try you can't seem to find your way out?

I know I have been down that black hole many times and it's no fun. I found I couldn't function normally, I couldn't think rationally, and I was severely depressed. Sometimes these episodes could last for months. As time went on, they lasted weeks and then days and then only hours until finally they disappeared altogether. If, early on, I had just taken my pain and sorrow to the Lord I wouldn't have been stuck in that black hole for so long.

I have talked to many others that have had this same feeling. I think it's the downward cycle of the roller coaster ride we are on. The downs are very scary and very depressing. I remember feeling myself starting to go down into the darkness, and I seemed unable to stop myself. I have since learned how to cry out to God. I now read God's Word and keep praying until I feel myself coming out of the darkness.

There is only one way out of the black hole that you find yourself in and that way is through God. He is there to support you through the most difficult times. God is bigger than any crisis that comes into your life. God is always there to carry you when you can no longer walk on your own. He is there when things get so bad you feel you can no longer go on. God will always be there to rescue you. You no longer have to spiral down that black hole without the hope of not being able to come back out. God is there to carry you out and bring you back into peace and comfort.

Today's Prayer

Dear Lord,

I am crying out to You today because I feel myself falling into the darkness. I'm scared and in pain. Lord, please rescue me from this horrible blackness. I know that You alone are my strength, and I can do nothing without You. Please pick me up and carry me, for my load is too heavy for me and I feel as though I'm sinking. Thank You for Your promise of peace, comfort and joy. Thank You for being the wonderful God that You are. Amen.

41

Time

"I am God your healer."
Exodus 15:26 (The Message)

"Then they cry to the Lord in their trouble, and He delivers them out of their distresses. He sends forth His Word and heals them and rescues them from the pit and destruction."
Psalm 107:19-20 (Amplified Bible)

I used to hate it when people would answer my question of "When does it stop hurting?" with, "Just give it time." That seemed to be the answer for everything, time. I wanted a better answer than that. I wanted something more constructive than waiting it out. Even our marriage coach told me that time was the answer. I knew that there was a healing process that I had to go through but even knowing this I still felt that my pain would never go away. After a while, I found that time alone did not heal my pain. It really does take much more than waiting for time to pass by to become healed.

At the beginning I thought the best thing to do was to wait and let time pass by. At every D-Day anniversary I assumed that I should be better because another year had passed. I found that every year that passed that I was still hurting and in pain. I began to realize that time alone was NOT going to heal me. I needed more than just time, I needed God. I needed to actively work at rebuilding my marriage. I needed to put all of my time and effort into our relationship if I wanted it to survive this massive hit.

I want you to know that it's okay to feel like the pain is never going to go away. Take comfort in knowing that the pain will not last forever. How you feel right now shouldn't be your main focus. I know it sounds impossible but try to keep your focus on staying close to the Lord and not turning away from Him. If you stay close to God, and nurture your relationship with Him, one day you'll say to yourself, "Hey, the pain isn't as bad as it once was." God is the source of your healing. You must make the commitment to keep your relationship with the Lord strong despite your inner turmoil.

Today's Prayer

Dear Lord,

I hurt so much, and all I want is to stop hurting. I know the pain won't last forever, but sometimes it feels like it will. Help me to keep my focus on You and not my pain. I want to draw close to You because I know that You alone are my source of healing. I make the commitment today to keep our relationship strong despite how I am feeling. Thank You for being the wonderful God that You are. Amen.

42

Hour by Hour

"Desperate, I throw myself on you: you are my God! Hour by hour I place my days in your hand, safe from the hands out to get me."
Psalms 31:14-15 (The Message)

"Don't panic. I'm with you. There's no need to fear for I'm your God. I'll give you strength. I'll help you. I'll hold you steady, keep a firm grip on you."
Isaiah 41:10 (The Message)

When I first found out about my husband's affair, I was living moment by moment. My mind was numb and I couldn't grasp what was going on. The pain was extremely intense and devastated is the only way to describe it. But, as time went on, I found that instead of moment by moment I was now living hour by hour, but the pain still seemed just as intense. As more time went by I started living day-by-day, and then month-by-month, until I was finally just enjoying my life again. The pain eventually does fade away, but as we know it was not just the fact of time passing by that was healing me and making me whole again.

I found that, no matter how long it's been, I would always carry some of that pain with me. It may not be intense or forthright but it's there in a sad kind of way. I find that emotions and triggers I have already dealt with can come flooding back at the most unexpected times.

This doesn't mean that it happens often, or that it is very intense, but still, it happens. But they don't scare me like before because now I know that I can throw myself at God's feet, and place the pain into His hands. I know that I am safe as long as I draw closer to God.

Have you ever been surprised at how things turned out in your life even though you had a different plan in mind? God is never surprised. He is your Master Planner and He has a set plan for your life. You don't need to know the details of His plan for you, all you need to do is walk with Him, fully trusting that His plan for your life is better than any plan you have for yourself. If you are unclear about where you are to go next, take time to read the Word, pray and meditate so that you can hear God's voice and know in which direction to turn next.

Today's Prayer

Dear Lord,

Sometimes I just don't understand what is going on and I feel so lost and confused. I am crying out to You, Lord, for sometimes I can only live hour by hour. Thank You Lord that You know exactly what is going on in my life and that all I have to do is put my full trust in You and walk in the direction You point to. Help me to put my full faith in the plans You have for me and not the plans I have for myself. Please reveal to me the next step I am to take. Thank You for being the wonderful God that You are. Amen.

43

Holidays

"Why are you down in the dumps, dear soul? Why are you crying the blues? Fix my eyes on God— soon I'll be praising again. He puts a smile on my face. He's my God. When my soul is in the dumps, I rehearse everything I know of you."
Psalms 42:5-6 (The Message)

You are going to find that every holiday, no matter how small, is going to be a trigger for you. My husband's affair lasted for an entire year so this was very true for me. Even if he spent that holiday or occasion with me, the holidays still bothered me for a very long time. Believe it or not, even the harvest season bothered me! Autumn is my favorite time of year, yet I couldn't get into it like I used to. You will find that holidays are hard because you are remembering or envisioning what your spouse did with the other person during these times. The gifts and cards they exchanged can be extremely hard to get past but not impossible.

Holidays and special occasions can cause us to trigger and be in tremendous pain. We should plan for this ahead of time knowing that these special days will be hard for us. Before the day even starts, dive into the Word and draw strength from it and be comforted by the words you read. Try to make the day extra special for just you and your spouse by making new traditions. But please don't get overly stressed out trying to make the day perfect. The quieter you can make the day, the better it will be for you. Plan your holiday time with only immediate family, if you feel that extended family and friends will add more stress for you. Remember that simpler is better.

When you feel yourself going down that black hole becoming depressed and angry, the solution is to look to God for help. You don't have to go through these special days alone and hurting. Cry out to the Father and put your hope in Him. Always remember Him when your soul is hurting. Know that this too shall pass, and you will soon be praising God with a smile on your face, because you know that He is the one that brings your healing, peace, comfort and joy even in the face of such sorrow. Pray and ask God to give you a wonderful plan for the holiday. His plans are always perfect, be sure to obey Him when He gives you a task.

Today's Prayer

Dear Lord,

I cry out to You, Lord, when again I am in pain and broken hearted. I will learn to depend on You and to praise You even when I am feeling such sorrow. Please help me get through this holiday with a renewed spirit and a peace within my soul. Please give me the plans you wish for me on this holiday. I know tomorrow is a new day, and I will be praising You again! I will fix my eyes upon You during this difficult day. Thank You for your perfect plans for my life. Thank You for being the wonderful God that You are. Amen.

44

Mourning Your Marriage

"I'm not saying that I have this all together, that I have it made. But I am well on my way, reaching out for Christ, who has so wondrously reached out for me. Friends, don't get me wrong: By no means do I count myself an expert in all of this, but I've got my eye on the goal, where God is beckoning us onward—to Jesus. I'm off and running, and I'm not turning back."
Philippians 3:14 (The Message)

I remember the day when I realized my marriage would never be the same again. The marriage I knew was now dead, and nothing was ever going to change that fact. I cried soul wrenching sobs when this realization came crashing down upon me. I then realized that I had a decision to make. I could try to live in the past and fantasize about what it used to be like, or pick myself up, dust myself off, look forward and make a new future for myself. For a while I tried the first option, but as time went on, I knew that living in the past wasn't going to get me where I wanted to go. I had to face the fact that my marriage had been forever changed, but that didn't mean it had to stay horribly painful.

I have spoken to many others that have felt the same way and they too were mourning the loss of their marriage as it once had been. It's fine to remember the good times and cherish the memories you've had in your marriage, but you need to live each day moving forward.

Focus on the kind of marriage you want and how you can get it there. You know that you can't go back to the past, no matter how much you want to. You also know you can't stay where you are. Who would want to be stuck in such pain anyway? That only leaves going forward, and this is the direction you need to be heading.

A Christian life is not stationary. When you walk with God you move forward into a more profound life with Him. Reach out for Him as He is reaching for you. Keep your eyes on your goal, and let God lead you. Turn your face toward your future, and see what God has in store for you and your marriage. God wants you to have a happy life and a happy marriage, He will not steer you wrong. Do what God is telling you do to in your life and marriage, no matter how hard it may seem. You will never regret obeying His command because obeying God will bring blessing into your life.

Today's Prayer

Dear Lord,

Please take me by the hand and lead me through every moment of today. I am utterly broken and I am crying out to You, Lord, for You are the Master Healer. I am committing to only looking and moving forward in my marriage. Thank You for reaching out for me while I am so broken. Thank You for being the wonderful God that You are. Amen.

45

Being In Control

"So letting your sinful nature control your mind leads to death. But letting the Spirit control your mind leads to life and peace."
Romans 8:6 (NLT)

Do you find yourself policing your spouse? Do you check up on them all day long? Do you constantly go through cell phone records, email accounts, bank or credit card statements, wallets, purses, computers, etc.? Do you find yourself doing these things all day long just to keep yourself sane? Are you doing these things instead of what needs to be done? Do you feel like your life will spin out of control if you don't do these things?

You will want to do these things to make sure the affair is really over, but after a while the intense policing does have to stop. Even though doing these things makes you feel better, it isn't healthy for you, your spouse or the marriage in the long run. Your spouse has to expect this type of behavior for a while, but no spouse wants to be picked over with a fine-tooth comb 24/7. I fully believe in having no secrets between spouses but there are better ways to go about it.

When your life feels as though it's spinning out of control, you may find yourself trying to hold on to whatever control you can grasp. You'll find that doing this will give you a sense of control not only in your life, but over your emotions too, but beware because it's a false sense of control. Being angry, broken, bitter, and just plain hurting is no fun and feeling out of control can make these emotions seem a hundred times worse.

You need to realize that God is the one in control, not you. No matter how hard you try, you still aren't in control, and you will drive yourself crazy trying to be. You need to learn how to release control. Give the control back to God, and let Him have the full control. I can promise you, you will always lose if you try to control it all yourself. Tell God that you are tired of fighting and that you are now giving Him the reigns over your marriage. The more time you spend with God, the more you will hear from Him and He will tell you all the things you need to know about your spouse and your marriage.

Today's Prayer

Dear Lord,

I am tired of fighting for control in my life and marriage. I want to release all control over to You. Please take my marriage in Your hands, and lead me on this road of recovery. Please show me how to let go of the control and to learn to take my lead from You. Thank You for sending me the Holy Spirit to guide my mind and to lead me toward a more peaceful life. Thank You for being the wonderful God that You are. Amen.

46

Society's Response to Grief

"My thoughts are nothing like your thoughts," says the
LORD. And my ways are far beyond anything you could
imagine. For just as the heavens are higher than the
earth, so my ways are higher than your ways and my
thoughts higher than your thoughts."
Isaiah 55:8-9 (NLT)

Have you found yourself trying to look and act normal when out with family and friends? I fought with this when I first found out. I couldn't seem to plaster a smile on my face and pretend that I was fine. I was no good at covering up my emotions. I would have strangers come up to me and ask if I were okay. Anyone looking at me could tell that I was NOT okay. I am not very good at hiding how I am feeling.

Do you find yourself thinking that you have to do pretend that everything is just fine? Why is it that we have to pretend that everything is okay when clearly it is not? Do you notice that society has a way of making us feel like we have to keep up appearances, maintain a certain way of living and cover up problems, as if pretending will somehow make things alright?

Sometimes we want others to think our lives are rosy and perfect, but life just isn't like that. Don't let the world tell you that everything has to be rosy and perfect. Pretending will block your healing process and make it last so much longer. Don't live falsely instead be honest with yourself and others about your feelings. Especially with your spouse, being honest about how you feel is very important. It is also very important that you express how you feel without being critical, judgmental, mean or vindictive. The more honest you both are in how your feeling, the faster your healing journey will go. If you are not telling family and friends about the affair, just let them know there are problems and that you both are working them out. This way they know why you are so upset without revealing all the details.

How you view your marriage and your spouse isn't the way God views it. How you think and feel isn't how God thinks or feels. Once you grasp and understand this concept, draw close to God and really listen to His wisdom. Pray for the ability to view your marriage and spouse the way God views them. Pray and sit quietly and listen for His voice of wisdom. He will lead you in the way you are to go.

Today's Prayer

Dear Lord,
I know that only You understand my pain and my needs. Teach me how to be honest without being mean or vindictive, and to not hide behind a false façade, but to be truly honest with others on how I am feeling. Please let me see my spouse and my marriage the way you see them. Thank You for sharing Your wisdom about my spouse and marriage with me. Thank You for being the wonderful God that You are. Amen.

47

Hiding

"Jesus said to the people who believed in him, "You are truly my disciples if you remain faithful to my teachings. And you will know the truth, and the truth will set you free."
John 8:31-32 (NLT)

Do you find yourself pulling away from family, friends, and even your spouse when you are depressed and suffering? Sometimes when we are in pain, we want to be left alone, so we pull away from those that love us and want to help. I didn't want to go anywhere or see anyone for months after I found out about my husband's affair. I was happy never leaving the house and never answering the phone. I wanted to crawl under a rock and never come back out. But once I started talking with others that have gone through the same thing, and talking with counselors, I began to feel much better. I no longer wanted to hide.

We also followed our counselor's advice and went out, just the two of us, once a week. I went even when it was the last thing I wanted to do. Sometimes we both had a miserable time, but we kept at it and I am thankful that we did. For months, we would go to a comedy club every weekend. At least we were laughing together! Learn to find a way to have fun with your spouse, even if it's the last thing you feel like doing.

Please ignore the impulse to push people away. Others can give you comfort and encouragement that you desperately need right now. They can help you keep your focus, because there will be times that your emotions will consume you. They can help you restore some balance to your life when you feel so off kilter. Don't be enslaved by your emotions, face them with the honesty and find someone to talk them out with.

Honestly evaluate your emotions right now. What feelings and struggles have you had since the moment you found out about your spouse's affair? God wants to set you free from these crippling emotions that are making you withdraw from others, life and your spouse. In the book of John it speaks about how "the truth will set you free." You should read the entire book of John to read about God's teachings on truth. The more honest you are with yourself and others, the freer you will become.

Today's Prayer

Dear Lord,

I want to be set be set free, please show me the truth and the way I should go. I no longer want to withdraw from my family, life and marriage. Please help me with all the emotions I have raging through me, and bring on a feeling of peace. Thank You for being the wonderful God that You are. Amen.

48

Faith Brings Joy

"Therefore, since we have been made right in God's sight by faith, we have peace with God because of what Jesus Christ our Lord has done for us. Because of our faith, Christ has brought us into this place of undeserved privilege where we now stand, and we confidently and joyfully look forward to sharing God's glory. We can rejoice, too, when we run into problems and trials, for we know that they help us develop endurance."
Romans 5:1-3 (NLT)

There were many times when I was severely depressed. I couldn't even remember what being happy felt like. There was nothing I, or anybody else, could do to make me feel better. Have you been feeling this way? Can you imagine rejoicing while feeling this way? When I was suffering I couldn't imagine rejoicing in it.

Looking back, I now believe that going through the recovery process has changed me into a better person. I also believe that we now have a better marriage now than we did before because of all the hard work we have done, and continue to do. I fully believe that our problems and trials do develop our endurance and they draw us closer to God.

It was through God's grace that I was able to cope those first few months. I wanted to end it all, but something made me see that wasn't the answer. Even if you don't see or feel God's grace, it's always there helping you. Anytime we go through hard times in our lives, God's grace is there to help us deal with what lies ahead. Without His grace, I don't think I would have been able to cope with the whole recovery process.

Did you know that as long as you're a Christian, God's grace protects you and helps you in many ways? When you need it the most, God gives it to you. He blesses you with His magnificent and absolute grace. It's very hard for us to understand why many things happen, but all we really need to know is that God's grace is absolute. God wants to pour out His grace upon you; all you have to do is ask. Be as specific as you'd like and ask for a certain kind of grace and He will give it to you. Through God and earnest prayer, you can find something to rejoice in the Lord about.

Today's Prayer

Dear Lord,

I'm suffering so much and I don't know how much more I can take. I know I cannot go on without Your grace being poured out over me. Please send Your grace and comfort during this trying time. Please help me see the good in every situation so I may rejoice and give You the praise. Thank You for being the wonderful God that You are. Amen.

49

Seeking Help

"Then I realized that my heart was bitter, and I was all torn up inside. I was so foolish and ignorant—I must have seemed like a senseless animal to you. Yet I still belong to you; you hold my right hand. You guide me with your counsel, leading me to a glorious destiny. Whom have I in heaven but you? I desire you more than anything on earth. My health may fail, and my spirit may grow weak, but God remains the strength of my heart; he is mine forever."
Psalms 73:21-26 (NLT)

After about a month I realized I needed help. I was having suicidal thoughts that wouldn't leave me alone, and I was becoming severely depressed. I couldn't eat, I couldn't sleep, and I was pushing everyone away from me. I was withdrawing from life, and I just didn't want to feel the pain any more. It was a hard thing to do, admitting that I needed help, but it was the best thing I ever did.

Are you in a dark place where you are feeling totally overwhelmed? If any of these things apply to you, I highly recommend getting some professional help.

- Dependant on alcohol or drugs
- Recurring thoughts of suicide
- Totally withdrawing from everyone

- Still struggling with depression after several months

There is nothing wrong with seeking help. You will be able to get farther along in your healing process if you do. You can ask your pastor or a Christian friend for recommendations. You can use your local phonebook or the Internet. You can also find help at online infidelity forums, by connecting with other people that are in the same situation that you are in. You'll find that helping others also helps you. You will feel better about yourself, which leads to feeling less depressed.

No matter how depressed, bitter, angry or brokenhearted you become, God will never let go of your hand. He will always be there guiding you with His counsel and leading you to your awaiting destiny. Pray and meditate over finding a good counselor. The Lord will lead you to the right person for you. *Isaiah 38:20 (NLT)* "Think of it—the LORD is ready to heal me!"

Today's Prayer

Dear Lord,

Please show me how to recognize when I need to seek help for my depression, and give me the courage to seek it out. Please lead me to the right people to talk to and the right people who need my help. I know You are going to heal me and I thank You for that. Thank You for being the wonderful God that You are. Amen.

50

Give Up or Go On

*"Brothers, I do not consider myself yet to have taken hold
of it. But one thing I do: Forgetting what is behind and
straining toward what is ahead, I press on toward the goal
to win the prize for which God has called me heavenward
in Christ Jesus."*
Philippians 3:13-14 (NIV)

*"You've all been to the stadium and seen the athletes
race. Everyone runs; one wins. Run to win. All good
athletes train hard. They do it for a gold medal that
tarnishes and fades. You're after one that's gold
eternally."*
1 Corinthians 9:24-25 (The Message)

Between six months and a year, there were many
times I just wanted to give up, move out, call it quits and
run away. I'm glad I never followed through with these
thoughts though. Even though I had them for a long time,
I knew, deep inside, I would never give up and leave. I
knew I was in this for the long haul, and I would never just
give up and leave. I made that decision the day I found
out about the affair. I knew I still wanted this marriage,
and I was willing to work hard to keep it. I knew that if I
left, I would regret not trying to work it out. I would have
always wondered if we could have been able to work it
out. How many happy years together would I have thrown
away?

Are you truly committed to this journey? Are you willing to go down the hard bumpy road that leads back to a happier marriage than you've ever had? Are you ready to say, "Yes, this hurts deeply and I hate it, but I am going to press on?" You must tell yourself that no matter what (except abuse, another affair, or addictions) you are in this for the long haul; that you won't act on your emotions. When you feel like giving up and running away, know that with prayer and hard work these feelings will and do pass.

God will reward your genuine willingness to commit to this hard road you've chosen to travel. He will never abandon you. He is in this for the long haul right there beside you. God is your confidant, friend, comforter and Master Healer. Let Him carry you when you feel like giving up. Cry out to Him when you feel you can no longer take the pain. God is your healing salve, and He will cover all your wounds and heal them with His loving hands.

Today's Prayer

Dear Lord,

I am committing myself to the long haul knowing that You will never abandon me. Thank You for being my comforter and Master Healer. I know that You alone will get me to my end goal of a happy and fulfilling marriage. Please give me an open heart and spirit to hear what You need me to hear. Thank You for being the wonderful God that You are. Amen.

51

Do You Trust Him?

"You don't have enough faith," Jesus told them. "I tell you the truth, if you had faith even as small as a mustard seed, you could say to this mountain, 'Move from here to there,' and it would move. Nothing would be impossible."
Matthew 17:20 (NLT)

"Trust in the LORD with all your heart; do not depend on your own understanding. Seek his will in all you do, and he will show you which path to take."
Proverbs 3:5-6 (NLT)

Do you fully trust God? I wish I could say that I did from the get go, but I didn't. I blamed Him for what was happening in my life. I thought I could fix all my problems myself. I did try for a very long time but soon I realized I was making more of a mess than fixing my life. I couldn't make the pain go away and neither could my husband, even though he did everything he could.

Do you trust God in your marriage? Do you trust in Him to pull you through this horrifying ordeal? Do you think that you have all the answers and you don't need Him? Maybe you even blame Him for what is happening in your marriage. Do you really believe that He can do the impossible? You only need the faith of a mustard seed! That is extremely small and that is all you need for God to do miracles in your life and marriage.

You need to cling to God and put all of your trust in Him. You need to take all of your feelings and questions to God honestly and openly. Plead to Him. Cry out to Him. Confide in Him. Then, just trust, while resting in His loving arms. Have you got anything to lose? You are already in what you may feel is a hopeless situation. If you trust in God, and He doesn't come through for you, you really haven't lost anything at all, right?

I can assure you, if you doubtlessly trust and believe in God, He will come through for you every time. His love for you is greater than you can ever imagine and He is bigger than any problem you'll ever have. You have to give Him the chance to show Himself in your life. You will find that God will prove Himself faithful and true if you will let Him. Be prepared to see miracles happen before your eyes.

Today's Prayer

Dear Lord,

In my heart I truly know that You are the only one who has never let me down. I am going to cling to Your promise that You are never going to leave my side or forsake me. I am going to put my full trust in You and Your promises. I fully believe You are going to do miracles in my marriage. Thank You for being the wonderful God that You are. Amen.

52

Anger: Slow and Steady

"He who is slow to anger is better than the mighty, And he who rules his spirit, than he who captures a city."
Proverbs 16:32 (NASB)

I had a real problem with anger. My husband would disclose details of the affair, at my asking, and I would explode in anger all over him. It wasn't pretty. Sometimes I would let my anger fester for weeks and refuse to talk about it. I didn't know how to properly express my anger or any of my feelings. I was suppressing it, and then having it explode out because I was keeping it locked inside. I was like a pressure cooker without a release valve. I know this was a big factor in why our recovery took so long.

If you are angry a lot when discussing affair issues, your spouse will not be forthcoming with any details. They will be afraid of your wrath every time. The calmer you are, the more likely your spouse is to be honest and open with you. Please do not ask questions that you really aren't ready to hear the worst case scenario answer to. Only ask questions you know you can handle, this will make it easier on both of you.

Anger needs to be expressed, but it should be done slowly, not exploded upon anyone else, including your spouse. When you're quick to show anger you are most likely dealing with "I deserve this" and "your plan" type of thinking. When you're showing this kind of anger it's saying that you are still trying to be in control. Explosive anger can hurt you, your spouse and your marriage. It will also slow down your recovery.

We should strive to be like God who is "slow to anger." When you are slow to anger it gives you a chance to find the real cause of it, properly deal with it, and express it in a healthy manner. Always strive for honesty when discussing how you feel and your reasons behind those feelings. Honestly and calmly communicate with your spouse about your anger and your feelings around it. When you feel that your anger is becoming too much for you to handle, take it to God before you take it out on your spouse. Earnestly pray about your anger and really lean on God and let Him work in you to calm the anger and bring peace back into your soul.

Today's Prayer

Dear Lord,

I'm so angry and full of rage. Please help me to be slow to anger when speaking with my spouse. Lord, sometimes my anger is more than I can bear. I am learning to lean on You through these hard times. Please show me the right way to handle my anger. Thank You Lord for your wisdom and insight. Thank You for being the wonderful God that You are. Amen.

53

Anger: Is It Wrong?

"Go ahead and be angry. You do well to be angry—but don't use your anger as fuel for revenge. And don't stay angry. Don't go to bed angry. Don't give the Devil that kind of foothold in your life."
Ephesians 4:26 (The Message)

Anger, by itself, is not a sin. Being angry is not ungodly. What you do with your anger, however, can lead you to sin. Everyone I have ever spoken to, that has been betrayed, has felt, in some degree or another, angry. This is a very common emotion when dealing with affairs. After the shock wears off and reality sets in, you may very well find yourself very angry. Angry at God for letting this happen; angry with your spouse for having the affair and damaging the marriage; angry with the other person, because they knew your spouse was married, and didn't care; angry with everyone that knew, and never bothered to tell you. This list of anger triggers could go on and on.

Anger does need to be released, but in a way that benefits your recovery rather than sabotaging it. The wrong way to release your anger is to yell at someone with negative words, explode on them, throw fits or just lose control. The correct way to release your anger is being open and honest with how you are feeling in a way that is physically, mentally, and emotionally liberating. You can do this by telling God exactly how you feel, holding nothing back, dig deep and let it all out. You may also take your anger to a marriage counselor, pastor, or someone that won't judge or criticize you. This way you can safely vent your anger without hurting anyone. You may be more comfortable writing everything you are feeling on a piece of paper. Get it all out and keep writing until you can't write any more. Burn the paper when you have finished writing. I use this tactic a lot to help me through my anger.

You shouldn't "let the sun go down on your anger." That means you should deal with your anger as soon as it appears. Don't go to bed and try to forget about it hoping that a new day will make it all go away. Trust me; it will keep coming back—and with increased intensity. Take time to read the Word, pray and meditate letting God help you deal with your intense emotions. God can work miracles in your heart and He can give you a whole new attitude. You'll find that your anger is no longer there. Ask God to work in your heart and to give you a new way at looking at things.

Today's Prayer

Dear Lord,

There are many times that I release my anger the wrong way. Please guide me in the right way to release my anger, so that it is helpful to my recovery. Please help me to be open and honest about my anger and to never suppress it. Teach me to lean on You and to hear Your wisdom. Please change my heart and soften it so that anger cannot take root. Thank You for being the wonderful God that You are. Amen.

54

Anger: Losing Control of Life

*"There is a path before each person that seems right, but
it ends in death."*
Proverbs 16:25 (NLT)

*"A person without self-control is like a house with its doors
and windows knocked out."*
Proverbs 25:28 (The Message)

You are probably trying very hard to gain control
back over your life and marriage. But really there is no
controlling these things and the more you try the angrier
you can become. You must learn that God, not you, has
total control. For a long time I thought that I didn't need
God, that I could handle things by myself. I was in control
of my life and no one else was going to tell me what to do.
I figured that I knew better and I knew how to fix things all
on my own. Wow, was I wrong.

Do you expect your life and spouse to be a certain
way? I think, in one way or another, we all do, but what
happens when others don't meet our expectations? Most
likely we get angry. Do you expect God to be a certain way
or to do certain things? What happens when God isn't
doing what you want Him to do? Do you get angry and
blame God for the way things turn out in your life? This is
a very common reaction to any unmet expectation.
Usually what is under the anger are feelings of

disappointment, feeling unwanted, unloved, unimportant and rejected.

God has a plan for your life and marriage. His plan will be His and not yours. His timing will be His and not yours. You need to learn to put your faith in God and trust that His plan and timing are what's best for you. Give God full control over your life and trust that His way is the only way. You may think you have a certain way you want your life to go and it seems right to you but if you choose your way over God's it will only lead to misery. God may take you in a completely different direction but as you obey God, you'll find that His way was perfect and that you're much happier. You'll always be glad you obeyed His command. You may feel that you can handle your healing journey on your own but you will find that it will end up a failure. Learn to let go and let God; He will not take you down the wrong path. Have faith and lean on Him and you will find the happiness you have been searching for.

Today's Prayer

Dear Lord,

When I feel out of control, I become so angry. Please help me to lean on You instead of myself. Teach me how to give You control of my life so that I can have the strength to make this journey I am on. Show me the right path to follow so that I won't end up in misery and despair. Thank You for showing me the right direction to go in. Thank you for being the wonderful God that you are. Amen.

55

Anger: Be Honest With How You Feel

"Mum's the word," I said, and kept quiet. But the longer I
kept silence. The worse it got. My insides got hotter and
hotter. My thoughts boiled over; I spilled my guts."
Psalms 39:2-3 (The Message)

It can't be expressed enough how extremely important it is to be really honest with yourself, and your spouse, about how your really feeling inside. The more honesty there is between you and your spouse, the better your recovery will be. The less honesty there is the slower and more painful your healing recovery will be.

This step took me the longest to do, and I still have a very hard time being completely honest about how I'm feeling. I would much rather say, "I'm fine" when I'm not. I should be open about it, but I keep a lot inside. I'm a work in progress, but as long as I am moving forward then I know I am heading in the right direction. My inability to be more open about my feelings made our recovery much longer and harder than it ever should have been.

There are right and wrong ways of being honest with your spouse, especially if you are angry. I used to tell my husband all the horrible feelings I was having, and blamed them all on him. I knew I was hurting him, but I would justify what I was doing under the cloak of honesty. This isn't the right way of being honest about your feelings. This is just being mean. A good honesty statement would be "I feel _____ about/when _____. Like, "I feel devastated when I see "her" in town." You want to express your feelings without placing blame. Never say "you", always make "I" statements. Never use the word "you" in the last part of the sentence.

Don't keep your feelings to yourself. No matter where you are directing your anger you must be honest about how you're feeling. Even if you lie to yourself about your anger you are not fooling God. He knows how angry you are, and He knows why you are angry. Keeping silent about your anger and pushing it down deep inside will only make your anger bigger. This will end up hurting only you. Remember, being honest is the most important step in your healing journey. You can tell God every horrible angry thought you are having, remember, He already knows!

Today's Prayer

Dear Lord,

You know me better than I know myself. I truly want to heal my marriage, but I know I need help with my anger. Please show me how to be true and honest with my spouse and myself with all the feelings I have raging inside me. I know that You are the only one that can help me with this. Thank You for being the wonderful God that You are. Amen.

56

Angry with God

"I'm absolutely convinced that nothing—nothing living or dead, angelic or demonic, today or tomorrow, high or low, thinkable or unthinkable—absolutely nothing can get between us and God's love because of the way that Jesus our Master has embraced us."
Romans 8:38-39 (The Message)

A lot of people I talk with come right out and tell me how angry they are at God for allowing this to happen to them and their family. Have you had any angry thoughts toward God since you discovered the affair? Maybe you don't want to admit it, even to yourself. Don't be too hard on yourself. Just because you are angry doesn't mean you don't still love God. Just as when you are angry with a friend or family member, you still love and care about them. Just know that God didn't cause this to happen to you and that He is in no way punishing you for anything.

If you're angry with God, He knows all about it, even if you never show it or admit it. Since He knows all, you might as well be totally honest with Him. Go ahead and scream and yell at Him till you are totally spent and have nothing left. Tell Him everything you are feeling; hold nothing back. If you can do this, you will feel much better. Holding anger inside can make you miserable. You will find such relief in letting go of your anger. God will then take you in His loving arms and let you cry it all out. He loves you so much and it hurts Him to see you in so much pain.

Even though you're angry with God, He is still as faithful as ever. He will never abandon you, no matter how you behave, or how you feel towards Him. God will always love and cherish you. You are His child and He will never turn away from you. You can curse Him, scream at Him, and yet He will still be there, loving you just the same as before. You can take comfort in the fact that God's grace is never ending. No matter what goes on in your life, good or bad, He is always the same loving and caring Father He's always been. No matter how big your anger is, God is bigger. No matter how deep your anger runs, God runs deeper.

Today's Prayer

Dear Lord,

Right now I am so angry with You! Even though I am angry, I am also grateful that You are forever faithful. I now realize that nothing can come between me and Your love for me, even my own anger. For this, I am forever grateful. Thank You for your unending grace and love. Thank You for being the wonderful God that You are. Amen.

57

Anger: Source and Limits

"Fools vent their anger, but the wise quietly hold it back."
Proverbs 29:11 (NLT)

"Smart people know how to hold their tongue; their grandeur is to forgive and forget."
Proverbs 19:11 (The Message)

It took a long time before I realized that my anger was my problem and no one else's. It was up to me to make a choice about my anger. I could either let my anger control me, or I could deal with it once and for all. After a while I choose to deal with it and I became a stronger and healthier person for it. I just wish it didn't take me so long before I dealt with it.

For a long time, I felt it was fine to shower my rage all over my husband. He deserved it, right? Maybe in a way, he did, but how long can you or your spouse live like that? I was not practicing the art of quietly holding back. This doesn't mean to shove it down and burry it. It means not to scream and shout horrible things at someone. Your healing is stalled when you're imprisoned by your anger.

To really deal with your anger you must know its source. What triggers your anger? As soon as you feel angry, ask yourself what just happened to make you feel this way. Try keeping a journal so you can find the root of your anger. You should also find the limits of your anger. How far can your anger go before it goes too far? When you know where this line is, between far enough and too far, you will be able to release your anger in a healthier way for you, your spouse and your marriage.

There is nothing wrong with being angry, but you can't throw your anger around letting it go where it may. You must learn to control your anger. If this is a real challenge for you, pray and seek help. Take your anger to God and tell Him that without His help you are unable to control your anger. He knows your anger, and why it's there, so don't be afraid to be totally honest with God about it because, as you know, He already knows. Seek God out, for He is there to help you and carry you when you can no longer make it on your own.

Today's Prayer

Dear Lord,

Please grant me the wisdom to know when to quietly hold in my anger. Teach me how to communicate without venting my anger everywhere. I know this will be hard, but through You I know all things are possible. Thank You for being the wonderful God that You are. Amen.

58

Anger: Unchecked Can Lead To Bitterness

*"Watch out that no poisonous root of bitterness grows up
to trouble you"*
Hebrews 12:15 (NLT)

*"Lead with your ears, follow up with your tongue, and let
anger straggle along in the rear. God's righteousness
doesn't grow from human anger. So throw all spoiled
virtue and cancerous evil in the garbage. In simple
humility, let our gardener, God, landscape you with the
Word, making a salvation-garden of your life."*
James 1:19 (The Message)

Bitterness can and most likely will poison your
marriage. Bitterness never fixes relationships, or makes
your heart joyful. Bitterness will always put a halt on your
healing journey. Bitterness is not a friend. You need to
kick it out of your life. You will find that harboring
bitterness in your heart will only bring you great sorrow. If
you let anger fester in your heart and you don't properly
deal with it, bitterness will start to take root. This is no
way to live the rest of your life. I have seen those who
choose to hang onto their bitterness in the act of being
right. All they accomplished was to lose their spouse,
friends and family because they were so miserable to be
around.

I almost let bitterness become my friend. I was
angry, and I felt justified in my anger, as most of us do.

After three years of being angry and becoming bitter I realized I would have to choose between being miserable and right or happy and married. I realized that my anger and bitterness was killing what was left of my marriage. When you're faced with devastation and pain in your life, you can either become bitter about it or you can become better from it. Which way would you rather live?

I want to challenge you to let God work through you so you can become a stronger and happier person. If you will allow Him to, God will do amazing things in your life and marriage. If you don't let Him do His work within you, bitterness will prevent you from receiving God's grace. God's grace is His free gift to you and He wants you to have it. Take any bitterness you have to Him, and let God melt it out of your heart forever.

Today's Prayer

Dear Lord,

I don't want to live with bitterness ruling my life. Please help me remove all bitterness I have in my heart towards my spouse. Please reveal to me the good works You are doing in my marriage. Please help me to see my spouse through Your eyes. Teach me how I can be more compassionate and loving towards my spouse. Thank You for being the wonderful God that You are. Amen.

59

Anger: Moving On

*"Then Jesus said, "Come to me, all of you who are weary
and carry heavy burdens, and I will give you rest. Take my
yoke upon you. Let me teach you, because I am humble
and gentle at heart, and you will find rest for your souls.
For my yoke is easy to bear, and the burden I give you is
light."*
Matthew 11:28-30 (NLT)

*"Peace I leave with you; My [own] peace I now give and
bequeath to you. Not as the world gives do I give to you.
Do not let your hearts be troubled, neither let them be
afraid. [Stop allowing yourselves to be agitated and
disturbed; and do not permit yourselves to be fearful and
intimidated and cowardly and unsettled.]"*
John 14:27 (Amplified Bible)

෨ᔿᕙ

Maybe you're not in a place where you're ready to
move past your anger and bitterness, but if you are, be
prepared to totally commit to that decision. Make sure
you have given yourself the time and opportunity to slowly
vent your anger. Also make sure you have honestly
expressed all your feelings, good or bad, with your spouse.
Remember this has to be done without blaming and being
hurtful. With God's help, you can move past all the anger
and bitterness around the affair.

When you fully commit to moving past your anger
you will find it to be freeing and up lifting. Making this

choice doesn't mean you will never be angry again; it means you are committed to working on letting go of your anger stemming from your spouse's affair. Letting go of this anger doesn't mean that the affair was "okay" with you. You can forgive and move past the anger without accepting that the affair was ever "okay" because clearly it's not. Letting go means to no longer harbor any bad feelings towards your spouse. Forgiving in no way means that you condone what they did. Letting go of your anger is a work in progress, but as long as you stay committed and are always moving forward, your healing will come. One day you will realize that you no longer carry anger or bitterness in your heart towards your spouse.

Don't feel that your anger is a hopeless cause. You can't deal with anger alone. The most important thing you can do right now is to ask for God's help. Learn to cling to Him in your darkest hours. He knows how hard it is to control and move past anger. Anger can make you physically and emotionally exhausted, and it can be a huge burden for one to carry. Give your anger to God, and He will give you rest.

Today's Prayer

Dear Lord,

Only Your strength can get me past this horrible anger and bitterness that I carry in my heart. I want to give You this burden I carry because I can no longer carry it on my own. I come into Your arms for comfort and rest. Thank You for being the wonderful God that You are. Amen.

60

Blame

*"But when the Father sends the Advocate as my
representative—that is, the Holy Spirit—he will teach you
everything and will remind you of everything I have told
you. I am leaving you with a gift; peace of mind and
heart. And the peace I give is a gift the world cannot give.
So don't be troubled or afraid."*
John 14:26-27 (NLT)

Have you ever noticed how much we humans love
to pass blame? We feel that if we pass the blame it will
help us feel better about the situation. It makes the
problem someone else's so that takes us off the hook. No
matter how much you want to, you shouldn't place blame
anywhere, not even on yourself. Cast out the word
"blame". Focus on the here and now, and where you want
to go from here. Blaming others doesn't resolve anything,
and in no way promotes the healing process. Don't get
sucked into the blame game. Blame is a black hole that
sucks you down and leaves you no hope of getting out.

It's easy to blame others when it comes to affairs.
You may blame your spouse for doing this to you and your
marriage. You may blame the other person because they
seduced and chased after a person they knew to be
married. You may blame everyone that knew about the
affair but covered for your spouse and never told you
about it. You may blame yourself for not being the perfect
spouse. You may blame God for letting this happen to

your marriage and family. But you must learn to not place blame anywhere. What happened cannot be undone and there is nothing that can change that fact. Blaming others will not change the past, but it will hamper your recovery.

Blame makes it impossible to heal because it puts you in the victim role. You'll find that blame accomplishes nothing. God knows of your situation. He didn't design it, but He did foresee it. God is waiting for you with open arms to give you the peace and comfort you're searching for. God doesn't want you to be worried and trouble over blame. He wants you to move forward and fill you with His comfort and peace. Blame will never be able to offer you that.

Today's Prayer

Dear Lord,

I know blame isn't doing me any good. It is only causing me more pain and it's keeping me from moving forward. Please send me Your comforting Holy Spirit to guide my thoughts and give me a clear perspective of my road ahead. I fall at Your feet, and ask You to please pour Your peace into my starving soul. Thank You for being the wonderful God that You are. Amen.

61

Bitterness and Resentment

"Don't pick on people, jump on their failures, criticize their
faults—unless, of course, you want the same treatment.
That critical spirit has a way of boomeranging. It's easy to
see a smudge on your neighbor's face and be oblivious to
the ugly sneer on your own. Do you have the nerve to say,
'Let me wash your face for you,' when your own face is
distorted by contempt? It's this whole traveling road-show
mentality all over again, playing a holier-than-thou part
instead of just living your part. Wipe that ugly sneer off
your own face, and you might be fit to offer a washcloth to
your neighbor."
Matthew 7:2-5 (The Message)

    I had a really hard time around other couples
watching them be happy while my husband and I were
miserable. Watching other couples hold hands, kiss, and
have fun together caused me so much pain and anger. I
found myself thinking, "Why couldn't it have been them
instead of us? Why did this have to happen in our
marriage? My marriage wasn't supposed to be like this."
I felt that it just wasn't fair. Why was God doing this to us?

    Have you found yourself thinking this way? If you
let this kind of thinking take hold, it will turn into
bitterness and resentment. Frustration leads to anger,
and anger reverts to bitterness. You may not even realize
that you've slipped into a resentful attitude. We are all
bound to feel this way at some point or another. You can't

avoid having these emotions but it's how you respond to them that determines if you are going to heal and recover fully, or not. If you don't deal with the issues behind your feelings you will be heading down a path of bitterness and resentment.

Bitterness can put you in a detrimental relationship with God. Bitterness actually causes a wall to come up between you and God. Maybe you're blaming Him for the way your marriage has turned out and that He is punishing you for some reason. This thinking is extrememly wrong because the bible says God is not ony tremendously in love with you, but His love is constant and unconditional. With God's help you can change your focus and attitude, and with this change comes a change of heart. God can change your heart and do wonderful things in your life. The best way to fight off bitterness and resentment is to diligently pray for a change of heart. God wants to take away all your bitterness and resentment and replace it with joy, peace and love.

Today's Prayer

Dear Lord,

Please forgive me of my bitterness and resentment. Please fill my spirit with peace, love and trust that I know only You can give. Thank You for never leaving my side, and for being there every time I need You. Thank You for being the wonderful God that You are. Amen.

62

Bitterness and Depression

*"So don't worry about tomorrow, for tomorrow will bring
its own worries. Today's trouble is enough for today."*
Matthew 6:34 (NLT)

*"Anxiety in a man's heart weighs it down, but an
encouraging word makes it glad."*
Proverbs 12:25 (Amplified Bible)

When bitter thoughts would start in my mind, I
knew I was going down that black hole of depression that
wad so hard for me to climb back out of. When my bitter
thoughts started I found myself in a personal pity party
that literally could last for days on end. I couldn't seem to
shut off all the negative thoughts in my mind. Every time
bitterness crept in, depression was right there with it. My
bitterness was from not dealing with my pain and anger. I
was burying those emotions, and trying to pretend they
weren't there instead of working through them.

Do you know that the only person you are hurting
with your bitterness is yourself? Bitterness is the exact
opposite of hope, the supreme corruptor of faith.
Bitterness will take away your joy and will keep you
trapped in your past. Bitterness will have you averting
your gaze from God's mercy and grace and will have you
focused on how God and the people that matter most
have let you down. Don't allow thoughts of bitterness to
derail your healing journey the way I did.

The longer you hold onto your bitterness, the longer it will take to truly heal your heart. Whenever you notice bitterness coming into your heart, forsake it in the name of God. Make bitterness your sworn enemy. This is a spiritual battle going on in your mind, and you have to treat it as such.

With God there is hope in gaining freedom from your bitter and negative thoughts. Don't overwhelm yourself. Take on one bitter and negative thought at a time. Pray for the strength to remove them the moment you notice they are there. Tell yourself that you are not going to go there. Remember to live in today, and think of all the positive things in your life right now. Do not dwell in yesterdays or tomorrows. God will deliver you from all your negative thoughts. All you need to do is ask, receive and have faith.

Today's Prayer

Dear Lord,

I have been fighting this battle on my own and I am failing miserably. I need You by my side because only with You will I have the power to win. Teach me how to live in the moment and show me things to be thankful for. Please release me from my bitter thoughts and replace them with positive ones. Thank You for all You have done and will do in my life. Thank You for being the wonderful God that You are. Amen.

63

Regrets

"To put off your old self, which belongs to your former manner of life and is corrupt through deceitful desires, and to be renewed in the spirit of your minds, and to put on the new self, created after the likeness of God in true righteousness and holiness."
Ephesians 4:22-24 (ESV)

In the months following D-Day, I kept saying things like, "I should have......" or "If only I........." or "What if........." I spent hours with these thoughts, regretting what I did or didn't do. There were many things I wished I could go back and do over. I have heard the same regrets from others suffering from their spouse's affair. This is a common feeling shared among those suffering the effects of infidelity. Living in the state of regret made me very depressed.

You can't beat yourself up thinking about the things you did wrong or what you could have done differently. The past is past and you can never change what has already happened. These things aren't going to bring you healing. Whatever you did or didn't do is now over and done with. Learn from it, and let it go. Be extremely aggressive in taking all thoughts of regret and worry captive. Do not allow them to steal your peace of mind. When worry again tries to take over your thoughts after you have already let them go, get ruthless.

When you find that your negative thoughts won't leave you alone read God's Word. Just let it soak it in, and meditate on verses that bring you peace and comfort. His Word is very powerful and it will help you conquer your negative thoughts. Pick an uplifting verse and repeat it when negative thoughts invade your mind. Try very hard to find all the good and positive in the world. If you make a habit of turning to God's Word for comfort, He will replace your negative thoughts with positive ones.

Call upon the Lord today. Look for, expect and hope in Him. The Word promises us that when we live in expectancy, when we stay hopeful, when we make ready for all the goodness of God, we will rise higher. Our strength will be renewed and we will overcome the trials in our lives. Get up each morning knowing that God is going to turn this all around. Stay hopeful and positive and in doing so God has promised to lift you up into the strength and victory He has waiting for you.

Today's Prayer

Dear Lord,

Please set me free from all regrets that I have been carrying around inside of me. Teach me to replace my old negative attitude with a new attitude of Christ-like behavior and prayer. Thank You for being the wonderful God that You are. Amen.

64

Depression

"Anyone who meets a testing challenge head-on and manages to stick it out is mighty fortunate. For such persons loyally in love with God, the reward is life and more life."
James 1:12 (The Message)

I suffered with severe depression for a good year after I discovered my husband's affair. It was so bad I couldn't function, so I sought out help from counseling and anti-depressants. Medication really helped me, but that doesn't mean that it's the answer for everyone. It helped me so that I could function throughout the day. I do believe everyone in this situation should seek out counseling, and consider medication if it is recommended by your doctor or therapist. Doing so will help tremendously.

Depression is very common when healing from affairs. I haven't met anyone that hasn't suffered from some kind of depression when dealing with infidelity. During this time it's nice to know that you are not alone in the way you are feeling. I find it comforting to know that Jesus also suffered from depression. He knew exactly how I felt. His most dear friends betrayed Him in His darkest hour of need. Read **Mark 14:32-42**.

Going through many different emotions is part of your recovery process. Never lose hope. Take one step at a time, and continue to put all your faith in God. When your depression becomes overwhelming lean on God and He will carry you in His strong loving arms until you are able to walk again on your own. Seek out people you can talk to and that will help you gain some emotional stability.

If your depression lasts longer that 6 weeks or you are having serious thoughts of suicide, I urge you to seek help. Talk to a Christian counselor, your pastor, or your doctor. Take action to find help for your depression. If one avenue fails try another. Keep trying until you find the right help for you. Never be embarrassed to ask for help because everyone goes through rough spots in their lives. Be sure you spend time reading the Word, fasting and praying about it. God will bring the right person to you, and lead you down the right path.

Today's Prayer

Dear Lord,

I am mindless and immobile in the midst of my depression. I know that You, too, have felt what I am going through. Please help me see that my depression is natural for someone in my situation, and help me to realize that it's okay to feel this way. I know that with You, I can withstand this trial. Please help me to find the right path and give me the strength to walk down it. Thank You for being my rock on which I stand. Thank You for being the wonderful God that You are. Amen.

65

Depression: Two Kinds of Losses

"Thanksgivings will pour out of the windows; laughter will
spill through the doors. Things will get better and better.
Depression days are over."
Jeremiah 30:19 (The Message)

"ARISE [from the depression and prostration in which
circumstances have kept you--rise to a new life]! Shine
(be radiant with the glory of the Lord), for your light has
come, and the glory of the Lord has risen upon you!"
Isaiah 60:1 (Amplified Bible)

Depression is directly related to the losses you
have experienced as a result of finding out about your
spouse's affair. There are two kinds of losses you can
have: concrete and abstract. The concrete losses you can
measure like you lost your spouse to death, lost your
income, lost your best friend, loss of a child, etc. The
abstract losses you can't measure and they include the
loss of your dreams, loss of affection, loss of your self-
esteem, loss of expectations, etc. The two types of losses
are both important, and you need to grieve them just the
same. The bigger your loss is, the bigger your depression
will be.

You will find that you only really grieve over
something when it meant a lot to you. My marriage was
my world so this was very devastating. I had to grieve
over the marriage that once was because I knew that my

marriage would never again be the same. You also need to let yourself grieve over your marriage that once was. Whether you realize it or not you have sustained a major loss. It can be dreams, self-image, what you thought was real, or even who you thought your spouse was. You will need to figure out everything you lost so that you can grieve and process each one. Healthy grieving is a very important part of your healing process. Just be sure you're always moving forward. Don't become stuck in your grief be sure your goal is to always move towards healing.

Don't think that God is testing you to see if you will stay faithful to Him. God is actually proving to you how faithful He is to you. Each day look to see how God will use your depression in your life. He can take this awful thing and turn it into something good. You may not see it now, but it is the truth. I have seen many people use their hardships to help others and become stronger people. Put your faith and trust in the Lord and know that you will come out of this depression a happier and whole person.

Today's Prayer

Dear Lord,

I am so depressed and I feel like all the peace and joy are gone from my life. I cry out to You, Lord. Please use my depression and turn it into something good in my life. Make me a better person because of it. Please help me to grieve all my losses and help me to move forward in my healing journey. Thank you for being the wonderful God that you are. Amen.

66

Depression: Devise a Plan

*"He came to a lone broom bush and collapsed in its shade,
wanting in the worst way to be done with it all—to just die:
"Enough of this, GOD! Take my life—I'm ready to join my
ancestors in the grave!" Exhausted, he fell asleep under the
lone broom bush. Suddenly an angel shook him awake and
said, "Get up and eat!" He looked around and, to his surprise;
right by his head was a loaf of bread baked on some coals and
a jug of water. He ate the meal and went back to sleep. The
angel of GOD came back, shook him awake again, and said,
"Get up and eat some more, you've got a long journey ahead of
you." He got up, ate and drank his fill...and it gave him
strength."*
1 Kings 19:5-8 (The Message)

If you devise a plan, you're going to find that it's
much easier to overcome your depression. You need to
have a strategy for this time in your life. You need to know
what you're doing and why you're doing it. Right now you
might not have the energy to do the things that have to be
done. You have to take care of your kids, your job, the
house, and you need to have a plan for dealing with all
these things.

Write out everything that you need to accomplish.
Even things like washing the dishes, sweeping the floor,
taking the kids to school. For the first six months my
memory was no longer working so I knew I couldn't rely on
it. Not to take a shower, not to eat, not to sleep, not to

make dinner, not to clean the house or do laundry, not anything! My mind was so focused on the affair that nothing else mattered. I wish I knew to write things down, even the smallest things, because it would have made a huge difference. Though I wonder if I would have remembered to read the list.

This is an extremely difficult time; so don't forget to take care of yourself. Action taken to complete a goal, no matter how small, will help you overcome depression. If you don't make a plan you will just add to your confusion and stress.

In our verse today you can see that Elijah was so depressed he actually wanted to die. But God had different plans for him. God wanted him to eat. You must be sure you're taking care of yourself right now. This is God's plan for you. Be sure you eat, drink and sleep. Don't do any of these things in excess. Pray throughout your day and have quiet time with God, so He can feed you spiritually as well. You can't do this without Him.

Today's Prayer

Dear Lord,

Please help me through this awful depression. Help me to devise a plan so that I am able to keep up with all my responsibilities. Please help me to keep You at the very top of my list, and help me to grow in You daily. Please bring to mind up-lifting verses for me to meditate on throughout the day. Thank You for being the wonderful God that You are. Amen.

67

Depression: Stop Your Negative Thoughts

"Summing it all up, friends, I'd say you'll do best by filling your minds and meditating on things true, noble, reputable, authentic, compelling, gracious—the best, not the worst; the beautiful, not the ugly; things to praise, not things to curse. Put into practice what you learned from me, what you heard and saw and realized. Do that, and God, who makes everything work together, will work you into his most excellent harmonies."
Philippians 4:8-9 (The Message)

One of the hardest things for me to learn was how to control my negative thoughts. To this day I still struggle with this. Once they started, they went on for hours and even days. Your negative thoughts are fuel you're your depression. If you want to overcome depression, you must learn to take control over the negative thoughts whenever they occur. Negativity worsens, and lengthens, depression. You must try to focus on positive things to change your thought pattern. One negative thought will breed another so try to think of positive things. These positive thoughts will in turn breed another and so on.

When I realized that negative thoughts were causing my depression to stay, and even get worse, I started keeping a gratitude journal. My gratitude journal was where I would write down all the things I was grateful for, or that made me happy (it can be about anything). I wrote in it every day. When I found myself starting to be sucked in by negative thinking I pulled out my journal. I read it over and over until I felt better and was no longer in a negative frame of mind. Maybe you have music that helps pull you out of a negative frame of mind. Find things that help you keep the negative thinking at bay and keep them readily at hand so you can have access to them when triggers happen.

Negative thoughts are almost impossible to conquer alone. You need to hand your negative thoughts over to God. He can replace your negative thoughts with ones that are positive. Meditate and pray while you read the Word of God. This, and a gratitude journal of your own, will help you overcome negativity. Memorize scripture that really speaks to you and brings out the good feelings inside of you.

Today's Prayer

Dear Lord,

I want to place all my negative thoughts in Your hands right now. Please replace these negative thoughts with ones that are positive and bring on good feelings. Help me to keep my focus on all the blessings You have given me. I hand over my depression over to You, Lord. Thank You for releasing me from my negative thoughts. Thank You for being the wonderful God that You are. Amen.

68

Depression: Get Rid of False Beliefs

*"....When he (Satan) lies, he speaks his native language,
for he is a liar and the father of lies."*
John 8:44 (NIV)

*"God created human beings; he created them godlike,
reflecting God's nature."*
Genesis 1:27 (The Message)

I remember feeling fat, ugly, unlovable, unwanted, and undesirable as a woman. I felt like a complete failure as a wife. Thinking these things didn't make it true, but at the time it felt as if they were true. My self-image had been shattered and I was very open to believing all these lies about myself. These thoughts caused me to hate myself, which in turn caused me to start hating everything and everyone.

Satan loves to whisper lies to us and it's up to us to see them for the lies that they are and not take them as truth. I had to learn that just because my husband had an affair that didn't mean that I was any less desirable. It didn't mean that I was unlovable, unwanted or ugly. I was letting my husband's affair shape who I thought I was and this was the wrong thing to do. I needed to see myself threw God's eyes, not man's.

Underneath your depression are beliefs. Beliefs like, you're unwanted, or you're not worthwhile, or you're not lovable, or you're not good enough. These are irrational beliefs and they are not based on reality. You need to challenge these thoughts, and if you don't challenge and deal with these false beliefs you are going to add fuel to your depression. Do not let Satan win; unmask these false beliefs with the truth. If you are unsure of what is true ask God. He will reveal the truth to you.

You need to look at yourself through God's eyes and see yourself as the worthwhile, lovable, and very wanted person that you are. God made you in His perfect image. You need to base your thoughts on the truth of God's Word and come to see yourself the way He does. Measure your self-worth through God, and no one else. God never lies.

Today's Prayer

Dear Lord,

Please help me to realize these negative beliefs are lies from Satan, and help me to ignore them. Open my heart and ears to hear the wonderful and pleasant truths about myself. Please let me see myself through Your eyes and help me to devise a new belief system about myself. Thank You for loving me so unconditionally. Thank You for being the wonderful God that You are. Amen.

69

Depression: Be Willing to Set Limits

"Now I take limitations in stride, and with good cheer..... I just let Christ take over!"
2 Corinthians 12:10 (The Message)

"Now God has us where he wants us, with all the time in this world and the next to shower grace and kindness upon us in Christ Jesus. Saving is all his idea, and all his work. All we do is trust him enough to let him do it. It's God's gift from start to finish! We don't play the major role."
Ephesians 2:7-8 (The Message)

You need to set limits on what you can and can't handle right now. When you are dealing with depression you don't want to live outside your physical, emotional and spiritual limitations. You may find this very difficult to do. You may feel like you have to keep up appearances and try to handle everything. Keeping up appearances causes more stress. You can only handle so much. Being in this mental state is extremely draining on your energy level. Your mental and physical limitations will be less than normal. Lower your expectations to match the new limitations until you have fully recovered.

When I was struggling with deep depression I decided that the best thing for my boys at the time was to put them in the local Christian school. I had always homeschooled them, but I was struggling so much that I realized that I wasn't able to school them the way they should be. So, I made the very hard choice to put them in school so I could focus on getting better. Sometimes you have to do drastic things but you need to get where you can focus on getting better. You need to be willing to set limits for yourself in everyday activities, and draw boundaries when you need too. Be willing to see the things that you cannot handle on your own or are just physically not able to do.

If you aren't sure what limitations you should set, seek God and pray about it. Ask the Lord to show you what you should let go of or change in your life right now. It will be difficult, and it may even make others upset, but put your trust in the Lord for He knows what is best for you. Remember that the Lord has only the best in mind for you and your family. He won't let you down. So be sure to obey Him quickly when God tells you to do something. You will never be sorry that you did.

Today's Prayer

Dear Lord,

I know I need to set limits in my life right now, please help me find what I need to set limits on. Help me to accept the limits You wish for me right now for I know it's so I can better handle the things in my life right now. I give You all of my worries, and I ask that Your will be done in my life. Thank You for being the wonderful God that You are. Amen.

70

Depression: Yes, There Is an End

*"......And be not grieved and depressed, for the joy of the
Lord is your strength and stronghold."*
Nehemiah 8:10 (Amplified Bible)

*"You have made (Or You will make) known to me the path
of life; you will fill me with joy in your presence, with
eternal pleasures at your right hand."*
Psalm 16:11 (NIV)

I found myself wondering if the depression would
ever end. I thought it would never go away. I learned that
it can be a very painfully slow process, but as time goes
by, and with the help of God, counseling, and close
friends, depression does get better. I have seen those in
my local support group go from dead inside to smiling and
laughing. It doesn't happen overnight, but it does
happen. I watched them move forward and through their
depression. Once someone laughed right out loud and
said, "Wow, I can't believe I just laughed!" We all laughed
and nodded because we all knew exactly what she meant.

At the beginning you feel dead and cold inside, like
you're void of any positive emotion. You need to move
forward and out of your depression even if it's only one
moment at a time. Sometimes I sat and looked at
something pretty, and enjoyed that one simple thing for
that moment in time. You can always find something, no
matter how small or insignificant it might be that you can

take joy from. It can be something tangible like a flower or something intangible like a good memory. Find some comedy movies and radio shows you can listen to. Find anything you can that makes you smile or even laugh. Allow yourself to forget for a while and just have fun.

The Lord is your joy and strength during this low time in your life. Know that you do not have to go through this alone. God never wanted you to go through this, but He is there to lift you up and even carry you if need be. He wants you to be whole again, and He is more than willing to pour His love and comfort into your spirit. Remember, God has created you for a purpose. Your life has meaning and worth through Him. You are very special in God's eyes.

Today's Prayer

Dear Lord,

I feel like I have been depressed for so long and that there is no end in sight. Please send hope back into my life again. Show me all the little things that can bring me joy even for just a moment. I know with You by my side, I will make it out of this depression. Thank You for being the wonderful God that You are. Amen.

71

Unresolved Emotions and Isolation

"Then I realized that my heart was bitter, and I was all torn up inside. I was so foolish and ignorant. I must have seemed like a senseless animal to you. Yet I still belong to you; you hold my right hand. You guide me with your counsel, leading me to a glorious destiny."
Psalms 73:21-24 (NLT)

"It is God who arms me with strength and makes my way perfect."
2 Samuel 22:33-34 (NIV)

❧

If you're not expressing your emotions, you are adding to your problems. You need to share your story with others going through the same thing. You also need to hear stories from others in similar situations. When you start helping others, you will feel better about yourself. Helping others puts your own life into perspective. You do not need to be fully recovered to help others going through the same thing. They can use your help and support from right where you are today.

I run a *Beyond Affairs Network* (BAN) support group here in NE Ohio, because I know how important it is for us to help each other. When I searched for a support group there were none around. I desperately needed one, so I decided to start one. Search for an infidelity support group in your area. If you can't find one in your area please start one. Go to www.beyondaffairsnetwork.com for more information on finding or starting a support group. It may be the best thing for your recovery. If you can't find a group, and you don't have the courage to start one, pray about it. God will bring the right people to you that you need in your life right now.

Your steps through this healing journey may be hesitant baby steps, but, as difficult as going down this road is, God wants you to move through your pain. Not around it, over it or under it, but through it. This is the only way to truly recover and come out the other side with your heart healed. Spend time in God's presence every day; tell Him everything you're feeling. He is always there and ready to hear you and comfort you in your time of need.

Today's Prayer

Dear Lord,

Please don't let me isolate myself. I know I need others around me for comfort and support. Please bring the right people into my life that I need right now. Please bring those that I can help into my life too. I am eager to lend help to those that need it. Thank You for being the wonderful God that You are. Amen.

72

How Are You Feeling?

"So, what do you think? With God on our side like this, how can we lose? If God didn't hesitate to put everything on the line for us, embracing our condition and exposing himself to the worst.... Do you think anyone is going to be able to drive a wedge between us and Christ's love for us? There is no way! Not trouble, not hard times, not hatred, not hunger, not homelessness, not bullying threats, not backstabbing, not even the worst sins listed in Scripture."
Romans 8:31-37 (The Message)

Going through such an emotional upheaval can really take its toll on your body. You can have stomachaches, headaches, joint pain, anxiety, digestive problems, rapid pulse and an overall heaviness. You may be eating everything in sight, or not eating at all. You may be having problems sleeping or sleeping up to 16 hours a day with nightmares plaguing you. You might be extremely fatigued and barely making it through the day counting down the hours till bedtime. I spent a few months in this state. I couldn't seem to be able to eat food. I couldn't turn my mind off so I could sleep. I found that I was in this hyper vigilant state of awareness for quite some time.

How you feel physically has a lot to do with how you feel emotionally. You need to take care of yourself physically so that you can start to feel better emotionally. You need to eat healthy food even if you don't feel like it.

Drink plenty of water, be sure to exercise and get at least 8 hours sleep a night. Remember, you are on a journey of healing for both your physical and emotional self. Take one day at a time if you need too. I remember a time when I had to take it one moment at a time and remind myself to breath. Be good to yourself, and don't think you should be any further along than you are right now.

Remember to face each problem with the affirmation of God's Word. His Word is full of promises for you; all you need to do is claim them for yourself. God is the Master Healer and He wants to heal you both physically and emotionally. If you remain faithful, you will be triumphant over every trial that you come up against while you travel down this road of recovery.

Today's Prayer

Dear Lord,

Please make me victorious over my physical problems. I know I can conqueror them with Your help. I know that with You by my side, I cannot lose. I am glad that no matter what happens in my life You will always be there for me and that nothing can take You away from me. Thank You for being the wonderful God that You are. Amen.

73

Satan Is Attacking

"The thief's purpose is to steal and kill and destroy. My purpose is to give them a rich and satisfying life."
John 10:10 (NLT)

"Keep a cool head. Stay alert. The Devil is poised to pounce, and would like nothing better than to catch you napping. Keep your guard up. You're not the only ones plunged into these hard times. So keep a firm grip on the faith. The suffering won't last forever. It won't be long before this generous God who has great plans for us will have you put together and on your feet for good. He gets the last word; yes, he does."
1 Peter 5:8-11 (The Message)

Satan loves to tear families apart. I believe it's one of his top priorities. Know that the tearing down of your family is not the work of God, but of Satan. God is not punishing you in any way. He did not design what is happening in your marriage even though He did foresee it. God is here to help and comfort you, not bring you harm. Satan is out to kill, steal and destroy. Any guilt or blame you hear in your head is Satan lying to you.

I'm sure your feeling overwhelmed by your emotions and maybe even on the verge of an emotional shutdown. I had the feeling that my future would be full of nothing but despair. Don't believe these lies. Your future holds hope and promise as long as you hold tight to your faith in God.

Those who don't believe in God don't view their problems the same way as Christians do. Non-Christians don't have God living inside them giving them the power to improve and have hope for their future. You have that option. You can choose to have faith in the Lord and from that choice you are choosing hope and a better future.

Make it a habit to give all your negative emotions to God. Picture yourself handing them over to God so He can deal with them. This is what God wants you to do. He doesn't want you to carry around all that negative baggage. He wants you to lay it all at His feet and to leave them there. Don't pick them back up. *1 Peter 5:7 (NLT)* *"Give all your worries and cares to God, for he cares about you."*

Today's Prayer

Dear Lord,

I am continuously distraught by my thoughts and emotions. I want to give each and every one over to You. I lay all my burdens at Your feet. Thank you for healing me and giving me strength to move forward. Thank You for being the wonderful God that You are. Amen.

74

Forgiveness

"Then Peter came to him and asked, "Lord, how often should I forgive someone who sins against me? Seven times?" "No, not seven times," Jesus replied, "but seventy times seven!"
Matthew 18:21-22 (NLT)

"Then he took a deep breath and breathed into them. "Receive the Holy Spirit," he said. "If you forgive someone's sins, they're gone for good. If you don't forgive sins, what are you going to do with them?"
John 20:22-23 (The Message)

What is forgiveness? I see forgiveness as getting your heart right with God. You do this by making the conscious choice to forgive others, and accepting God's forgiveness for yourself. Forgiving your spouse doesn't mean you are relieving them of the responsibility around the affair. Forgiving your spouse also doesn't mean you automatically trust them either. Trust is something they need to earn back. I believe forgiveness is letting God's love flow through you.

Forgiveness is a very hard step but a necessary step in rebuilding your marriage after infidelity. It was a choice I had to make every day. In no way are you freeing them from their responsibility around the affair if you choose to forgive them. What you are doing is handing over the responsibility to God. You know that your spouse has to someday answer to God. Forgiveness is your obedience to God. Forgiveness is saying that you will no longer harbor anger, bitterness or resentment toward your spouse.

Forgiveness is not about feelings. It's not about forgetting. It's not about pretending it didn't happen. It's not about trusting your spouse. It's really not about reconciliation. Forgiveness is a purposeful decision you make to obey God.

Forgiveness is also a process that takes time. It doesn't happen overnight if it does, it's not true and complete forgiveness. When you forgive, you are letting God take over and letting Him work on your spouse. You put a wall up between you and God when you choose not to forgive. When you're free from the pain, anger and hatred, and you are experiencing God's peace, you know you have truly forgiven.

Today's Prayer

Dear Lord,

I know that it is only through You that I can completely forgive my spouse. Please help me from destroying our relationship, and myself, with my unforgiveness. You know this is the hardest thing I've ever had to do. Thank You for sending me Your strength. Thank You for being the wonderful God that You are. Amen.

75

Forgiveness: It's Your Choice

"In prayer there is a connection between what God does and what you do. You can't get forgiveness from God, for instance, without also forgiving others. If you refuse to do your part, you cut yourself off from God's part."
Matthew 6:14-15 (The Message)

"And become useful and helpful and kind to one another, tenderhearted (compassionate, understanding, loving-hearted), forgiving one another [readily and freely], as God in Christ forgave you."
Ephesians 4:32 (Amplified Bible)

As I've said before, forgiveness is a choice you make. You will likely have to make that choice over and over again for a while. People like to mistake forgiveness as something they should "feel" before they can forgive. However, forgiveness is a choice, not a feeling. People, who say they can't forgive, aren't willing to forgive.

Forgiveness is a purposeful decision you make to obey God. No one can make you forgive your spouse. Not your spouse, not your friends, not your family, not your pastor and not even God can make you forgive. God gave us free will, and this is the time to use it. It's your decision. The fate of your healing journey lies in your hands. It's all up to you now.

If you choose not to forgive, you will grow anger and resentment in your heart turning it hard against God. Your quality of life will suffer, along with your relationship with God and your spouse. Without forgiveness, there can be no intimacy in your marriage.

Forgiving is a way of releasing ourselves from our own prison of bitterness. God doesn't want to see you trapped in a prison of your own making. Forgiving someone of infidelity is no easy task. I could not have done it on my own. It was only through God that I could forgive my husband and move forward to a happier marriage.

Today's Prayer

Dear Lord,

Please help me to forgive my spouse. I feel that I cannot do this without Your help. Please remove any bitterness and hatred I may have in my heart towards my spouse. Give me a forgiving heart, and help me to move forward in my healing. Thank You for being the wonderful God that You are. Amen.

76

Forgiveness: The Catalyst to Healing

"Make allowance for each other's faults, and forgive anyone who offends you. Remember, the Lord forgave you, so you must forgive others."
Colossians 3:13 (NLT)

"And whenever you stand praying, if you have anything against anyone, forgive him and let it drop (leave it, let it go), in order that your Father Who is in heaven may also forgive you your [own] failings and shortcomings and let them drop."
Mark 11:25 (Amplified Bible)

To forgive is to heal. It restores you and makes you whole. Forgiveness will bring you peace and joy as it leaves behind your guilt and shame. Forgiveness gives you back your life. All the negative feelings you carry around about your spouse's affair will consume you, if you let it. The longer you hold onto them the more you'll die inside. God does not want you to live in pain and misery. He wants you to live in prosperity and happiness.

So why choose to forgive? Because you will find that the pathway to having peace of mind is forgiveness. Trying to get through your spouse's infidelity is anything but peaceful. My mind didn't stop going over the affair non-stop for at least 6 months. Peace of mind doesn't come all at once. As you work through the forgiveness process you will find that your peace of mind comes back to you gradually.

The thoughts of the affair were tormenting me. I felt like they were literally killing me. I couldn't even remember what peace and joy felt like. I remember crying out to God because my very soul was dying. This was no way to live, and I just couldn't take it anymore. I decided it was finally time to truly forgive.

Being a Christian doesn't mean we can't find hate in our hearts. When we find it, we must give it over to the Lord. He is able to search out your heart and bring you to forgiveness, if you will just be obedient to His Word. It absolutely doesn't matter what has been done to you or how much you have suffered, God still wants you to forgive so that you may enjoy the life He has given you. The key to life's enjoyment is forgiveness.

Today's Prayer

Dear Lord,

I so badly want to heal both emotionally and physically. Please help me forgive my spouse for their infidelity. Please set me free from these awful thoughts and feelings around the affair. My soul is so heavy, Lord, please send me Your comfort today. Thank You for loving me unconditionally. Thank You for being the wonderful God that You are. Amen.

77

Forgiving the Other Person

*"You're familiar with the old written law, 'Love your friend,'
and its unwritten companion, 'Hate your enemy.' I'm
challenging that. I'm telling you to love your enemies. Let
them bring out the best in you, not the worst. When
someone gives you a hard time, respond with the
energies of prayer, for then you are working out of your
true selves, your God-created selves. This is what God
does. He gives his best to everyone, regardless: the good
and bad, the nice and nasty. If all you do is love the
lovable, do you expect a bonus? Anybody can do that. If
you simply say hello to those who greet you, do you expect
a medal? Any run-of-the-mill sinner does that."*
Matthew 5:43-47 (The Message)

Forgiving the other man/woman is one of the
hardest things to do. It's so easy to place all the blame on
that other person. They most likely knew your spouse was
married, but didn't care. We can come up with all sorts of
reasons to be angry with the other person and place the
blame with them. Forgiving the other person can
sometimes take much longer than forgiving your spouse.
For some it could take years, especially if the affair
partner is a close friend or family member.

This is a very important step in your healing
journey. Harboring anger towards the affair partner will
cause bitterness and resentment to grow in your heart,

just as harboring anger towards your spouse will. Not forgiving the affair partner will halt your healing process.

Forgiveness is letting go of your pain, anger and the need to get even. Some of us don't want to forgive because we still want to have the "right" to be angry with someone over what has been done to us. When you quit hanging on to the pain, you will find your healing. Remember, forgiveness is about you, not the other person. You don't need to physically say anything to them or ever even see them in person to forgive them. It really doesn't have anything to do with them; it really is about getting your heart right with God and letting go.

God tells us to forgive each other as He has forgiven us. He does not want us to judge others for their actions after we have forgiven them. He no longer wants us to hold anything against them. God wants you to forgive the other person, because He knows if you don't there will be a wall up between you and Him. He won't be able to help and guide you like He wants to if you choose not to forgive.

Today's Prayer

Dear Lord,

Please help me forgive the other person. I know You love them as much as You love me. Please set me free from the pain surrounding the other person, and give me a forgiving heart towards them. Lord, this is so hard, please give me strength. Thank You for being the wonderful God that You are. Amen.

78

Forgiveness Will Set You Free

"Forgive us our debts, as we also have forgiven our debtors."
Matthew 6:12 (NIV)

"Judge not [neither pronouncing judgment nor subjecting to censure], and you will not be judged; do not condemn and pronounce guilty, and you will not be condemned and pronounced guilty; acquit and forgive and release (give up resentment, let it drop), and you will be acquitted and forgiven and released."
Luke 6:37 (Amplified Bible)

How can you tell if you have truly forgiven? I could tell because I could feel God's love flow through me and out towards my husband. When he walked into a room I could just feel it. It was actually wonderful to feel this way again. There was a time, when he walked into a room; all I felt was rage, hatred, betrayal, bitterness and resentment. None of those feelings are very freeing. I would rather have love in my heart than those other dark emotions. Knowing that I have truly forgiven my husband is extremely freeing.

If you can't feel God's love flow through you towards your spouse, or you think they don't deserve your forgiveness, or if you think you just can't forgive yet, you must dig deeper. I've heard that forgiveness is like an onion as it has many layers. Forgiveness isn't complete until you've gone through all the layers. When you have fully forgiven, then you are free from your self-induced prison. Unforgiveness hurts only you. By not forgiving someone, you are willingly keeping all those negative feelings inside you, making yourself miserable.

God's Word is clear, just like Christ has forgiven us when we have sinned against Him, we also must forgive those who have sinned against us. This is your key to unlocking the prison door and setting yourself free once and for all from the hurt and pain the affair has caused you. God doesn't want you to be trapped in your self-made prison. He is there waiting to set you free. Forgiving infidelity is one of the toughest jobs God will ever call you to do. It is not easy, natural, or simple. All you need to do is ask for His help and guidance and He will gladly give it to you. He is waiting for you with loving arms opened wide.

Today's Prayer

Dear Lord,

Please give me the strength to forgive so that I might free my heart to fully love again. I realize that I must forgive just as You have forgiven me. Thank You for loving me enough to die for my sins. Thank You for being the wonderful God that You are. Amen.

79

Forgiving Yourself

"I remind you, my dear children: Your sins are forgiven in Jesus' name."
1 John 2:12 (The Message)

"If we claim that we're free of sin, we're only fooling ourselves. A claim like that is errant nonsense. On the other hand, if we admit our sins—make a clean breast of them—he won't let us down; he'll be true to himself. He'll forgive our sins and purge us of all wrongdoing. If we claim that we've never sinned, we out-and-out contradict God—make a liar out of him. A claim like that only shows off our ignorance of God."
1 John 1:8-10 (The Message)

Forgiving myself was extremely hard for me to do. I blamed myself for so many things concerning the affair. It was so bad that I started hating myself. I felt that had I done this, or that, differently the affair wouldn't have happened. I felt that had I paid more attention to the signs, and not been so trusting, the affair wouldn't have lasted as long as it did. Blaming myself was only making matters worse. I was becoming my own worst enemy, because I just couldn't seem to stop the blaming and forgive myself.

But you have to realize that even if you made mistakes (we all do) like having a bad attitude, were neglectful or did, said or thought inappropriate things, in no way did this give your spouse any right to have an affair. That was their choice alone. No one can make another have an affair. You have to realize that you didn't make your spouse go out and cheat on you. This was 100% their choice. You can take 50% ownership of the problems in the marriage but your spouse is 100% responsible for the affair. You need to learn to forgive yourself of the things you either did or didn't do. This was very hard for me to learn how to do. It actually took a couple of years to fully forgive myself, to let go and move forward.

You must decide to forgive yourself just as God has forgiven you, even if you feel you don't deserve it. Isn't it great that we don't have to measure up to any high standards to be deserving of His love and forgiveness? God loves you no matter what you have done. He knows you inside and out and He will always continue to give you His unconditional love and undying grace.

Today's Prayer

Dear Lord,

Please help me to forgive myself. Teach me to let go of the things I cannot change. Thank You for forgiving my sins and washing me in Your blood making me fresh and new. Thank You for being the wonderful God that You are. Amen.

80

One Step Forward, Two Steps Back

"We pray that you'll have the strength to stick it out over the long haul—not the grim strength of gritting your teeth but the glory-strength God gives. It is strength that endures the unendurable and spills over into joy, thanking the Father who makes us strong enough to take part in everything bright and beautiful that he has for us."
Colossians 1:11-12 (The Message)

Have you noticed that it feels like you're going backwards instead of forwards? More than once my husband has said to me, "It feels like we're right back at square one." It was very disheartening. Just when you think things are finally moving forward something will happen that sets you back. Maybe it is a new piece of information, a discovered lie, an attempt at contact, etc. These situations cause us to temporarily go backwards. Though it may seem hopeless at times because of the constant effort at trying to deal with it all, you will succeed because you have God on your side. Many times I wished I could just make myself forget this ever happened. My brain was tired of going over and over it, day in and day out.

Even though it may feel like your back to square one, in reality, you really are not. Recovering from your spouse's infidelity is full of ups and downs, but your downs never really go all the way back down to where you were on D-day. You may fall back a bit but you're still upward from where you were on that first day. When you're taking your hurts and fears to the Lord with a strong desire to move forward and you are learning about the healing process and applying what you have learned then you are making great progress.

God wants you to bring your fears and hurts to Him because He loves you more than you could ever imagine. God wants you to be totally healed and whole again. He wants to give you comfort and fill your soul with love and peace. God will make a way for you if you allow Him into the places where you hurt the most. He will heal your pain when you give all of yourself to Him. Through prayer, you can face your pain and fears with God's help.

Today's Prayer

Dear Lord,

I get so discouraged at times because it feels like I am going backwards more than forward. Please help me to quit worrying and trying so hard. Please be my strength and support during this difficult time. Lord, I place all my hurt and pain in Your hands. Thank You for replacing it with Your peace and love. Thank You for being the wonderful God that You are. Amen.

81

Destructive Choices

"Those who live only to satisfy their own sinful nature will harvest decay and death from that sinful nature. But those who live to please the Spirit will harvest everlasting life from the Spirit. So let's not get tired of doing what is good. At just the right time we will reap a harvest of blessing if we don't give up."
Galatians 6:8-9 (NLT)

In an attempt to escape the pain you may look for short-term solutions. Short-term solutions can be anything; drugs, alcohol, overeating, excessive shopping, or extra hours at work. Short-term solutions are destructive choices. They only create an "illusion" of dealing with the emotions that we have ranging inside of us. Eating a pint of chocolate ice cream, though very yummy, really isn't going to make anything go away because none of the issues have been addressed.

This type of behavior only makes your recovery that much longer, and it dishonors your values. When you engage in this behavior, you are only displacing your hurt and anger, not removing it from your heart. You also aren't facing your issues head on. Short-term solutions suppress the feelings, rather than allow you to deal with them openly and honestly.

My short-term solution was to throw myself into a project full force. It could have been a craft project, a yard project, a computer project or just any kind of household project. These projects kept me from thinking about anything else. I also would read every self-help book on affairs and forgiveness I could find and just study and read them over and over. Maybe I thought that by reading and knowing all this information it would magically make everything alright again. While these seemed productive at the time, it was only a temporary hiatus. The feelings were still there, they were just being masked by my "productiveness". Quick fixes only last a moment in time, and they are never a solution to your problems.

The only permanent solution is God, as He is forever. You want to work at pleasing the Spirit so that you will be able to move forward in your healing. If you seek to please the Spirit, you will produce the Spirit's fruit into your life and you will use the Spirit's virtues toward others. Learn to not just know about God but to really know Him in a deep and intimate way. Learn to get passionate about God and to seek Him out with all your heart.

Today's Prayer

Dear Lord,

I no longer want to sow my sinful nature. I want to sow seeds that please the Spirit. I have been in such pain for so long, please give me the strength I need to not give up. Keep me moving forward toward You. Thank You for being the wonderful God that You are. Amen.

82

Self-Esteem

"Others were given in exchange for you. I traded their lives for yours because you are precious to me. You are honored, and I love you. "Do not be afraid, for I am with you."
Isaiah 43:4-5 (NLT)

"What's the price of two or three pet canaries? Some loose change, right? But God never overlooks a single one. And he pays even greater attention to you, down to the last detail—even numbering the hairs on your head! So don't be intimidated by all this bully talk. You're worth more than a million canaries."
Luke 12:6-7 (The Message)

An affair can really wreak havoc on a person's self-esteem. We start doubting so many things about ourselves during this time. I know my own self-esteem took a nosedive. I felt that the other woman was thinner and prettier than I was, and way more fun to be around. I felt like I was no longer good enough. I liked who I was before my husband's affair, but after I found out I no longer saw myself as someone worth. I felt like my life no longer had any purpose and like someone had just thrown me in the trash.

When you obsess about negative self-thoughts your self-esteem will suffer and you'll start to feel worthless. Don't let those thoughts take a hold of you.

They are absolute lies whispered to you from Satan. In God's eyes you are a very valuable person. You must learn, as I did, that your self-worth is not based on how other people view you. If you do, you will feel unloved and unwanted.

Even though the pain is very real you cannot let this be the measuring stick for your self-worth. No matter what your spouse or anyone else says about you, don't let it have power over you and lower your self-esteem. This can be very difficult, especially if you've viewed your self-worth through your spouse or marriage.

God views you as a very lovable and wonderful person. God felt that you were so valuable that He sent His son to die for you. God's opinion of you is the only one that matters. He doesn't ever want you to think badly about yourself. Don't let those lies that Satan whispers to you take hold. Rebuke them in the name of the Lord and pray that God will fill you with self-worth.

Today's Prayer

Dear Lord,

Please help me to see how worthwhile I really am. Please help me to distinguish between what is true and what are lies being told to me by Satan. Thank You for loving for me so unconditionally and telling me how precious I am. I know that I am truly worthwhile. Thank You for being the wonderful God that You are. Amen.

83

Trust

"The LORD *says, "I will guide you along the best pathway for your life. I will advise you and watch over you."*
Psalms 32:8 (NLT)

"Trust God from the bottom of your heart; don't try to figure out everything on your own. Listen for God's voice in everything you do, everywhere you go; he's the one who will keep you on track. Don't assume that you know it all. Run to God!"
Proverbs 3:5-7 (The Message)

Trust is the glue that holds a relationship together. An affair shatters that trust. Never again will you have the same trust toward your spouse as you did before the affair, but maybe that is a good thing. I don't believe we should ever have a blind kind of trust towards our spouse's. This doesn't mean you will never trust your spouse again, but it will be a different kind of trust. Trust is extremely difficult to bring back after an affair. Not impossible, but very difficult. I believe that if it weren't for God, I would have NEVER trusted my husband again.

Even though, at the time, I no longer trusted my husband I knew that I wanted to stay married to him. You may be feeling the same way, but you may also be wondering how the trust will ever come back, and if it does how long does it take. Trust comes back very slowly. Just like the rest of the healing process, the trust won't come back overnight. It's also not going to happen just by your spouse saying, "You can trust me now." The only way they can prove to you that you can trust them again is to repeatedly show you through their *actions*. We all know that actions speak louder than words, and you are going to need a LOT of proven actions to begin trusting again.

Until your spouse has shown you through many actions that you can trust them again, you will have to learn to lean on God. When I had zero trust in my husband I was scared and full of anxiety. Horrible thoughts would plague me and the only way I found, at the time, was to police my husband night and day. I then learned that the only way I could combat the anxiety and fear was to pray and lean on God, knowing that He had my best interests at heart. God promises to guide, advise and watch over you all your life.

Today's Prayer

Dear Lord,

I want to be able to trust my spouse again, I just feel unable to right now. Please help me to learn to trust again. Guide me and show me wisdom for when I should trust and when I shouldn't. Thank You for guiding me, advising me and watching over me while I learn to trust again. Thank You for being the wonderful God that you are. Amen.

84

Moving Past the "Whys"

"If you don't know what you're doing, pray to the Father. He loves to help. You'll get his help, and won't be condescended to when you ask for it. Ask boldly, believingly, without a second thought. People who "worry their prayers" are like wind-whipped waves. Don't think you're going to get anything from the Master that way, adrift at sea, keeping all your options open."
James 1:5-8 (The Message)

"Keep on asking and it will be given you; keep on seeking and you will find; keep on knocking [reverently] and [the door] will be opened to you."
Matthew 7:7 (Amplified Bible)

Do you find yourself asking, "Why?" a lot? Why did my spouse do this to me? Why did my spouse do this to our family and marriage? Why did the affair partner do this to me? Why did my spouse have the affair?

There are many "whys", and if you let them they will drive you crazy. They spiral you further into that tunnel of depression. We might never really know all the answers to all the whys. But we have to realize that if we want to heal and move forward, we are going to have to eventually move past, and let go of, all the whys.

I got to the point that I stopped asking God "why" and started asking Him "how". Questions like, "How can I use this situation to help others?" or "How can I become stronger from this?" We must eventually change our focus off the whys and onto the how's. Doing this is a huge step in your healing progress. Pray and ask God how your situation can help heal others. As I've said earlier, helping others is a wonderful way to heal yourself too. God wants you to use your situation to help others that are hurting and going through the same thing.

God understands your strong desire to know the answers to all the whys. Pray that the Lord will take that desire away and put in its place a desire to know the answers to all the "hows". God can work miracles in your heart, and you will be pleasantly surprised to find that one day you really don't care about the whys anymore because you're too busy with all the "hows". You will feel a great sense of well-being knowing that you are doing God's work in helping others.

Today's Prayer

Dear Lord,

Please help me to accept that sometimes there isn't an answer to my "why" questions. Please take away my desire to know why and fill me with a desire to find out the hows. I am going to believe without doubt that the trust in my spouse will come back. Thank You for being the wonderful God that You are. Amen.

* Please visit my site www.godlywhispers.com and listen to the free MP3 of Pastor Carson Robson's sermon "Current Struggle – Future Self".

85

Personal Boundaries

"We can rejoice, too, when we run into problems and trials, for we know that they are good for us -- they help us learn to be patient. And patience develops strength of character in us and helps us trust God more each time we use it until finally our hope and faith are strong and steady. Then, when that happens, we are able to hold our heads high no matter what happens and know that all is well, for we know how dearly God loves us, and we feel this warm love everywhere within us because God has given us the Holy Spirit to fill our hearts with his love."
Romans 5:3-5 (TLB)

Before the affair, I had no idea what personal boundaries even were. From talking with others who had gone through this with their spouse's, I learned what healthy and unhealthy boundaries looked like. Knowing what they were and how to stand by them really helped me in my healing. Some of the boundaries you may need to look at are: Are you violating your personal values to make someone else happy? Are you letting other people direct your life and tell you how you should live it?

My husband and I learned what the unhealthy boundaries were and we learned how to turn them into healthy boundaries to help affair proof our marriage. These were things like:

- Not having a close relationship with someone of the opposite sex.
- Not discussing any type of marriage problem with those of the opposite sex.
- Being careful of what another person's motives are.

Keeping boundaries like these will help make your marriage more affair proof. This doesn't guarantee that there will never be an affair, but it will make both of you more aware of what can cause affairs to even start.

God wants us to have healthy boundaries in our marriage and all our relationships. If you aren't sure what those boundaries are, or what they should be, pray and ask God to show you. Through His wisdom and guidance God will help you find your healthy boundaries. He will help you find the right emotional, mental, physical and spiritual boundaries that will help you live a happier and productive life. In turn, you will have happier and stronger relationships including your relationship with God.

Today's Prayer

Dear Lord,

Please reveal me what my personal boundaries are, and please help me to stand by them in a Godly way. Thank You for reminding me that my problems and trials only make me stronger and more patient. Thank You for loving me and filling my heart with love and joy. Thank You for being the wonderful God that You are. Amen

86

Telling the Children

*"The Fear-of-God builds up confidence, and makes a
world safe for your children."*
Proverbs 14:26 (The Message)

*"The reverent, worshipful fear of the Lord leads to life,
and he who has it rests satisfied; he cannot be visited
with [actual] evil."*
Proverbs 19:23 (Amplified Bible)

My sons were 8 and 9 years old when my
husband's affair was disclosed. They were too young to
understand what was going on. All they knew was that
something major was wrong and that mom and dad might
get a divorce. They had no idea why, and I feel that is the
way it should be. They did not need to know the whys of
what was going on. An affair is adult business, and it
should be kept as such. Children who know something is
wrong do need to be reassured that you both still love
them very much; that even though mom and dad are
having some problems, it has nothing to do with them. If I
had to do it again, I would try my very best to make sure
they knew nothing was even wrong, but that isn't always
possible, and it can be extremely difficult.

I would advise, no matter how old your children
are, that you never disclose the affair if at all possible.
Even though you may really want to make your spouse
look horrible in your children's eyes, this should NOT be

done. They are going to know that something isn't right, and they will feel that it is their fault. Children have a way of thinking that their parent's problems are somehow their fault so please try and shield them as much as possible to the devastation that is occurring in your marriage. Never make your spouse look bad in the eyes of your children no matter how much you really want to.

Every situation is going to be different; as well as each child is different. There is no simple solution that will blanket everyone's situation. We must learn to seek comfort and guidance from the Lord. God will not let you down; you need to take your concerns about your children to Him, not your friends and family. When you pray, do so with a quiet heart and mind. He will lead you in the right direction concerning your children. Be sure to pray for your children, because they are hurting too.

Today's Prayer

Dear Lord,

I had no idea that my children would be facing these struggles. Thank You for the support that You will give them through all this. Thank You for sustaining us all through this hard time. Lord, please teach me to be loving, kind and compassionate so that my children will learn from my example. Thank You for being the wonderful God that You are. Amen.

87

What if the Children Already Know?

"Be strong. Take courage. Don't be intimidated. Don't give them a second thought because GOD, your God, is striding ahead of you. He's right there with you. He won't let you down; he won't leave you."
Deuteronomy 31:6 (The Message)

I have spoken to those whose children knew about the affair before they did. This is very sad and such a hard situation for a child to be in. Wanting to tell the parent but not wanting to hurt them, and not wanting to feel like the one that broke the family apart. What do you do in a situation like this?

If your children already know, make sure you are honest with them about what is going on. This doesn't mean they need to know all the details. Give them as little as possible without lying, and let them know what your intentions are. Make sure they are never in the middle of what is going on between your spouse and yourself. Just because they know doesn't mean that they should be mixed up in it. Never use your children as your person marriage counselor! Leave adult issues for the adults.

They need to know where mom and dad stand, and that mom and dad still love them. Children never want to see their parents split up and divorce. If you're not planning on going that route, be sure they know this. Let them know that no matter how bad it may look for a while that mom and dad are really trying to work things out. Let them know that neither of you are planning on leaving the other. Also, to help reassure them, you can talk about what you and your spouse are doing to work on the problems in your marriage, such as going to couples counseling. Always reaffirm your love for them, and reaffirm that they are not the cause of what has happened.

This is such a trying time in your life, but you don't need to feel intimidated and overwhelmed by it all. Having to deal with the aftermath of an affair with everyone confused, angry and hurt can be very disheartening. Take comfort in knowing that God is with your entire family every step of the way and Gods loving arms wrapped around your children. God is always right there beside you, and He won't ever leave you or let you down.

Today's Prayer

Dear Lord,

Please be with my children as they need You just as much as I do. Please give me the wisdom and strength I need to teach them how to cope and how to recover. Please show me how I can reassure my children that they are loved and very wanted. Thank You for being the wonderful God that You are. Amen.

88

God's Will in Your Life

"We are assured and know that [God being a partner in their labor] all things work together and are [fitting into a plan] for good to and for those who love God and are called according to [His] design and purpose."
Romans 8:28 (Amplified Bible)

"And your ears will hear a word behind you, saying, This is the way; walk in it, when you turn to the right hand and when you turn to the left."
Isaiah 30:21 (Amplified Bible)

Do you know that God has a plan for your? God wants to use you, so please let Him show you how. Two years into my recovery, I felt a calling to write this devotional. I kept telling myself that I couldn't write, and, in fact, I hated writing. But the thought kept coming to me. I struggled with this thought of needing to write this devotional for over 2 years.

Finally, after praying about it I knew I had to write it. I had never undertaken such a huge project like this before. I felt that God was calling me to do it and that the tugging at my heart to write one wouldn't go away until I finally just said yes. God wanted to take this horrible thing that has happened in my life and turn it around to help others that are in the same pain that I was once in.

Maybe you're praying and seeking God for His will in your life and you feel He isn't speaking loud enough for you to hear Him. Maybe you feel He isn't answering your prayers in the time frame you want them to be answered in. In today's world we all seem to want everything right now, but we have to remember that God moves in His own time, not ours. You must make sure that you don't use any "quick fixes" or believe you know the obvious answers to your prayers. Don't get ahead of God. You must be certain that everything you do follows God's perfect plan and timing for your life.

Every day, diligently listen and learn from God and His Word. He will never abandon you. God is always working for what is best for you in every part of your life. If you don't hear from God personally, He may use others to speak through. When you believe you know His plan, don't try and force it to happen. If you force it then it turns into your plan and not His. God will make His plan happen in His own way and time so just follow what God tells you to do when He says to do it.

Today's Prayer

Dear Lord,

I want to know Your will in my life, and I want to commit my life to You so that it can be used by You in accordance to Your perfect plan. Teach me to be still in prayer and to hear Your voice. Please help me to be patient for my answers to prayer. In waiting, I will be doing Your will. Thank You for being the wonderful God that You are. Amen.

89

Do You Have An Active Prayer Life?

*"Meanwhile, the moment we get tired in the waiting,
God's Spirit is right alongside helping us along. If we don't
know how or what to pray, it doesn't matter. He does our
praying in and for us, making prayer out of our wordless
sighs, our aching groans. He knows us far better than we
know ourselves and keeps us present before God. That's
why we can be so sure that every detail in our lives of love
for God is worked into something good."*
Romans 8:26-28 (The Message)

*"And we are confident that he hears us whenever we ask
for anything that pleases him. And since we know he
hears us when we make our requests, we also know that
he will give us what we ask for."*
1 John 5:14-15 (NLT)

You can't know what God is saying to you if you
only take the time to listen every now and then. Are your
prayers rushed and automated? Are the motives behind
your prayers completely self-serving? If you answered yes,
often or even sometimes, then you need to get more
active in your prayer life. You need to strive to have a
more personal relationship with the Lord. The more you
seek Him, the more He will seek you.

Don't just pray when you are at church. You need
to spend alone time with God every single day. Read the
Word, meditate and pray listening for God's voice. Pray

every day, morning noon and night. Make a habit of quieting your mind and listening for His voice. Pray when you wake up in the morning, as you do your daily tasks, and then again when you turn out the lights for bed. Make a habit of talking with God all day long in everything you do. God cannot do His will in your life if you do not meet with Him face-to-face daily. The more you seek His face, the more God will use you to reach out to others.

As it says in **1 Thessalonians 5:17;** "Never stop praying." What does this verse mean to you? Maybe it seems impossible to you. Do you tell yourself that you're too busy to stop and pray? Praying all the time doesn't have to be impossible. It's a habit you need to create in your life. The more you do it, the more you are going to want to keep doing it. The Holy Spirit lives in all those who love the Lord and God knows your hurts and struggles and the deepest desires of your heart. He wants you to live a rich and full life and you will start receiving many blessings once you become more intimate with God obeying His commands.

Today's Prayer

Dear Lord,

Please teach me to quiet my mind so that I may hear Your voice. Show me how to pray and give me reminders to pray often. Have the Holy Spirit fill and move through me and speak with the Lord in my behalf. Thank You for being the wonderful God that You are. Amen.

90

The Only Healing Relationship

"In all their troubles, he was troubled, too. He didn't send someone else to help them. He did it himself, in person. Out of his own love and pity he redeemed them. He rescued them and carried them along for a long, long time."
Isaiah 63:9 (The Message)

"See, I am sending an angel before you to protect you on your journey and lead you safely to the place I have prepared for you."
Exodus 23:20 (NLT)

There is only one relationship that will heal your shattered heart and that relationship isn't with your spouse; it's with Jesus Christ, the Master Healer. He knows what you are going through because He has experienced what you are experiencing right now. He is the only one that truly knows your suffering, devastation and grief. No matter how much you want your spouse to help; your spouse can't fully heal your broken heart. They can greatly help, but they cannot completely heal it.

This was something I learned the hard way. I expected my husband to heal my heart and take the pain away. When that didn't happen, I blamed him for it. This made our already rocky relationship even worse. I couldn't understand why I was still in so much pain when we seemed to be doing everything right to heal our relationship. Then I learned that people, no matter who they are, couldn't fill the hole I had in my heart. Only God could do that.

Don't make the mistake I did. Don't expect, or demand, that your spouse heal your broken heart and remove the pain you are in. This is asking something of them that they cannot give; no matter how hard they try. As your relationship grows with the Lord, you will see that He is the only healer. As your prayer life grows stronger, you will find the pain and brokenness of your heart is no longer as intense as it used to be. As time goes on, and your relationship with the Lord grows deeper, your heart will no longer be broken. You will once again be filled with peace and joy.

Today's Prayer

Dear Lord,

Help me to understand that only You can heal my broken heart and to not expect my spouse to do Your job. Let me find true healing in You, Lord. Only You know how truly brokenhearted I am and how much pain I am in. Please fill the hole in my heart and send Your healing today, Lord. Let me fall into Your arms and feel Your comfort. Thank You for being the wonderful God that You are. Amen.

Made in the USA
Lexington, KY
12 November 2014